GLORIA!

D1380815

GLORIA!

THE ARCHBISHOP'S WIFE

Abidemi Sanusi

Published 2014 by HippoBooks, an imprint of ACTS, Challenge Enterprises, WordAlive and Zondervan.

Africa Christian Textbooks (ACTS), TCNN, PMB 2020, Bukuru 930008, Plateau State, Nigeria. **www.acts-ng.com**, **www.actskenya.org**

Challenge Enterprises of Ghana, PO Box 5723, Accra, Ghana. **www.ceghana.com**

WordAlive Publishers, PO Box 4547, GP0-00100 Nairobi, Kenya. **www.wordalivepublishers.com**

Zondervan, Grand Rapids, Michigan 49530. **www.zondervan.com**

ISBN: 978-9966-003-23-2

Cover design: projectluz.com
Book design: To a Tee Ltd, www.2at.com

14 15 16 17 18 19 /DCI/ 18 17 16 15 14 13 12 11 10 9 8 7 6 5 4 3 2 1

CONTENTS

PREFACE

My prayer for those who will read this book is that through it they will find out that God can pick someone with a life like mine and transform it. Only Jesus Christ, the great life-changer, can do that!

This book can be called an account of God's faithfulness in a life that could have been described as a failure and a disappointment. I was physically and spiritually dead, and now, by the grace and mercy of God, I am physically and spiritually alive – although still very much an unfinished product.

This book does not tell everything that God has done for me. But it does tell some of the miracles he has done, even before I knew him. Thinking back over these events has left me amazed at how God looks after a life until he brings his purposes to bear in and through it. But looking back has also made me more aware of my own thoughts, strengths and weaknesses. I can only say that this book was written because God wanted it so. I never thought that my life would provide good material for a book, but here it is. This book has helped me to express myself. It has also helped me to reflect myself as one looks at a mirror.

I write on behalf of those who have gone through persecution and torture just because of their Christian faith. Many are not as privileged as I am to share their experiences, and their sufferings, but I know that God's presence is in the midst of all of their situations.

There are those who have no one to listen to their stories or lift their spirits. Some have lost their lives, some have become widows and widowers, some have been orphaned. I share my story with such people. I am a fellow pilgrim.

I do not want to take the grace of God for granted. The fact that I am alive today is only by his grace. Although, my experience lingers in my mind as if it were yesterday, it does so, not with unforgiveness but rather with gratitude to God, who protected, provided and healed me in every way, and also gave me strength for my everyday walk with him.

It is my prayer that the Lord will give you wisdom to grasp the lessons you need from this account of my life.

To Him be the glory.

Gloria Kwashi
God's daughter
Mother
Archbishop's wife

ACKNOWLEDGEMENTS

First of all, Gloria and I want to acknowledge the Lord God. It was he who took a girl from some obscurity and made her a wife, mother, teacher, preacher, inspirer and mother of many. It was he who spoke to her through Gbile Akanni's preaching on enlarging your tents, leading her to begin building the Zambiri School and put up extensions to accommodate the children in Gidan Kauna, the official residence of the Bishop of Jos. It was he who spoke to Sid Garland and Paul Todd of ACTS (Africa Christian Textbooks) and to Pieter Kwant, Isobel Stevenson and others associated with HippoBooks and the Langham Partnership, leading them to agree that Gloria's story should be told.

Her story was beautifully written by Abidemi Sanusi who lovingly entered our home, our hearts and our family. Her time with us will not be forgotten. She gleaned stories from friends, relations, children and anybody who knew anything about the Kwashi family. She travelled extensively in the Plateau State and in Adamawa State to learn the story of Gloria, the archbishop's wife.

We also thank Auntie Susan, our diocese, our co-labourers in all the places we ever served and the people whom we served.

We do not know how to thank God enough except by showing our gratitude by using our lives in his service.

FOREWORD BY BARONESS COX

Gloria Kwashi is one of my heroines for many reasons. Here, are three of them:

First, if you visit her home, you can see a three-dimensional picture frame filled with ashes and a metal cross twisted by fire. This is all that remains of one of her earlier homes, which was set alight by militants. She and her husband (also one of my heroes) had to flee, carrying their children with them. But Gloria and Ben continued their ministry, always under threat of similar violence.

Secondly, Gloria herself was subsequently attacked by militants, suffering horrendous brutality. But her courage and faith are inspirational. Whenever we meet, I am humbled by her radiant smile. When she and the members of her Mothers' Union worship, they do so with such vibrant, joyous faith that they seem to me to be living testimony to the truth that "God is a very present help in trouble".

Thirdly, Gloria's enormous capacity for love is shown by her ever-expanding family. In addition to her own children (now grown up), Gloria and Ben have adopted a large number of orphans and other children in need of care. They live in an extension to the Kwashi home. I cannot say how many there are as the last time I visited, a few weeks ago, several more children arrived and were welcomed into the "family".

With such courage, faith and boundless love, it is not surprising that my personal name for Gloria is "Gloria in Excelsis"!

Caroline (Baroness) Cox

FOREWORD BY THE ARCHBISHOP OF JOS

Writing this foreword is both difficult and easy. Difficult, because I am writing about a person I have loved, lived with, known and shared the most intimate part of my life with for over thirty years. Easy, because the book has been so beautifully written that reading it has brought tears to my eyes, laughter in my mouth, and much swinging of my emotions. I rejoice and am filled with gratitude to God for the gift of the wonderful life of Gloria.

The story of Gloria's birth, early life and how she came to be a mother to many homeless, vulnerable children and orphans is hardly known, even in Jos, Nigeria, where she lives. She does not talk about her work in the community. She hardly talks about her achievements, her travels and the places she has been across the globe. If you asked her to talk about herself, she wouldn't make any reference to the wonderful roles she plays as a mother, international speaker and evangelist.

I understand this, even if, sometimes, I am incredulous as to why she doesn't celebrate her achievements. Nothing is impossible with Gloria. She does not give up easily. She sees things way ahead and makes plans to accomplish them.

If our children and other members of our extended family who have passed through our home were each to contribute to this book, the stories they would tell about Gloria would be difficult to believe, yet they would all be true.

My wife is a gifted teacher and preacher. She has led revival meetings in Kenya, Uganda, and all over Nigeria. In 1998, she was a seminar leader at the Lambeth Conference, the global Anglican conference that takes place every ten years in the UK. As a young woman, she made presentations as a female theologian in Ghana, Ethiopia, Finland, Denmark and the US, to name, but a few.

One of the remarkable things about Gloria is the fact that she invested in our six children by homeschooling them until they were ready for secondary school. By the Lord's grace, all six are doing well and serving God. Hannatu is a doctor, Rinji a priest and missionary, Pangak an automobile engineering student, Arbet a medical student, Nendel a law student and Nanminen is in high school. Gloria is able to tell you the faith journey and confession of each child!

I am convinced that it is great women who make men great. I am further convinced that godly women alone have what it takes to raise children to become godly men and women. I learnt this from living and sharing life with Gloria – as this book will attest.

Ben Kwashi
Gloria's husband

1

MY ORIGINS

I was born on the roadside near a remote village in northern Nigeria on a market day in May 1958. My mother and her friends were going from village to village to buy food that they would later resell when she went into labour. They didn't have anything sharp to cut the umbilical cord, so they sawed through it with a corn stalk they found growing nearby. Then they washed me down with rain water, wrapped me in rags and carried me back to our village, near Numan town, in a basin.

I was so sickly that I turned blue (despite my dark skin!). No one expected me to live. Even my mother was so convinced that I was going to die that she didn't bother giving me a name.

But I hung on. My mother ended up taking me to a missionary clinic that was in my village. She had to keep on going back because although I wasn't dying, I certainly wasn't thriving. On one visit, she met a Fulani man who had brought his child to the clinic. That was unusual. The Fulani are nomadic cattle-herders who prefer to use traditional medicines rather than go to clinics. Hospitals are usually a last resort. They go there only when they are on their deathbeds.

My mother's people had a good relationship with the Fulani. Our languages are similar, and there was a lot of intermarriage with them even though the villagers were predominantly Christian and the Fulani were supposedly Muslim. They joined in our festivals and ate the same things we did. Some of them actually converted to Christianity. It's a shame that this friendship has been replaced with ethnic tensions in Nigeria today.

So anyway, this Fulani man took his child to the missionary clinic, and he found my mother there with a child like his on the verge of death. I was still wrapped up in the rags.

"What's that all wrapped up in rags?" he asked my mother.

"It's a child," my mother answered.

"Well, is it a boy or a girl?"

"It's a girl."

"What's her name?"

"She hasn't got one. And there is no point giving her one either, because she is probably going to die."

It sounds harsh, doesn't it? But my mother lived in the village where infant mortality was high. She loved me, but was also realistic about my chances of survival. I was very sick and could die at any moment. So what was the sense of giving me a name?

The Fulani pondered this – the child with no name. Then he asked my mother what day I was born.

"Sunday," my mother said. "Sunday."

"Then she'll be called *Ladi*, Sunday," the Fulani man pronounced.

My mother and her friends laughed, either at the name or at the Fulani man, I'm not really sure which. But then a miracle worked its way into that name. My mother said that every time I cried, she would say, "Ladi, be quiet!" and I would stop crying. I don't know how or why, but it seemed that whenever they called me that name, I grew stronger. Strength and life poured into my body.

Looking back with the knowledge I now have, I suspect that I probably had tetanus. I have seen other children with symptoms similar to those my mother said I had. Very few of them survive. It is a miracle that I am here at all!

So that is how I was named. By a Fulani man, a Muslim, who saw a nameless, sick child and named her Ladi – Sunday. In later years, I would change my name to something that I believed said more about me and God's grace in my life: Gloria. But at this point, I came to be known as Ladi, *Sunday*.

My Father, the Polygamous Soldier

I come from a tribe in north-east Nigeria called the Bachama. Well, we were known by that name when I was born. Now we are called the Bwatiye Bachama. The men of my tribe tend to be tall and solidly built and are known as warriors. So when the Biafran War broke out in 1967, my father, who was the son of the traditional ruler of our tribe, was one of the first to sign up to fight in the Nigerian army. I guess he was looking for adventure, the kind he couldn't get with a young family to care for. I was about nine at the time, but I can still remember the joyous shouts of the young men in the village at the prospect of war. Little did they know...

You may have forgotten about the Biafran War, but it was one of the bloodiest periods in Nigeria's history and still stirs up strong emotions in Nigeria today. It came just seven years after we became independent of the British in 1960. The country had come to be divided along ethnic lines, with the (mostly Muslim) Hausa and Fulani in the north, the (Christian/animist) Yoruba in the southwest and the (Christian/ animist) Ibo in the east. The east is also where Nigeria's main export, oil, is located. Increasing political tension eventually led the head of the eastern region, Colonel Emeka Ojukwu, to declare the independent Republic of Biafra, effectively removing the eastern region from the Federal Republic of Nigeria. But the other regions refused to allow it to secede. What followed for the next three years was the Nigerian Civil War, also referred to as the Biafran War.

During the height of the war, my grandfather passed away. His death left the Bwatiye council with a dilemma. According to the rules of inheritance, my father should have become the next traditional ruler. But he was away in the army and showed no inclination to come home. He had now travelled around Nigeria and gotten a taste of life outside our "backwater" village, and he wanted more. (Also, I believe, he didn't want to be shackled by the responsibilities of married life, so when he saw his chance to escape, he took it.)

So the elders decided to follow the Bachama tradition regarding what to do when a ruler died without a son. They turned to the eldest son of the next most senior clan and crowned my father's cousin paramount chief. He was never fully comfortable with this role and kept asking my father to take his rightful place as *Kpana Rigangyin*. When it became clear that my father wouldn't do so, he gave him the title of second-in-command of the kingdom. That was my father's title until he passed away.

My father's time in the army was not a good time for us. We didn't see him at all. My mother was left with ten children and effectively no husband. I am the fourth child in the family. I have three older siblings and six younger ones. The last child, number ten, was a boy from another tribe whom my mother adopted. That was my mother through and through. She didn't have much. Well, she had nine children and a husband fighting in the civil war. Yet, when she found out about that boy in need in a distant village, she didn't think twice about adopting him, even though things were really hard for our family.

My father married and remarried frequently. It was easy for him to do this because he was a prince and because of the traditional way people got married in the villages. If he saw a woman he liked, he would send a mediator to the girl's family to plead his case. If they all agreed, they would set a date for the wedding. Then, on the wedding day, the girl and her family would come to his home singing and dancing. He would hand over the dowry (a cow and whatnot) and she would become his wife. In my tribe, it didn't matter how many times the groom married; the bride still got a dowry and other gifts, even if she was the tenth wife. That is how my father was able to marry and remarry the way he did.

My childhood was punctuated by stories of my father leaving his wife in one village and then marrying another woman in another village or city. Soon, the wife he left behind would also marry someone else. That was village life. People did not divorce per se; they just separated. That is, they would go their separate ways, and if they found someone else to marry, that was exactly what they did.

As far as I can remember, my father always had at least two wives. The most wives he had at one time – that I knew of – was three. He was a nominal Catholic, but in those days, the Catholic Church didn't much care if people held on to their traditional beliefs as long as they went to church.

That hasn't really changed in some circles. Nigeria is a very religious society. However, even though some people may call themselves Muslim or Christian, what they actually mean is that they are nominal followers of that faith. In their hearts, their real faith is in traditional, animist beliefs.

My Mother, the Business Woman

My mother was a typical African woman in that she believed that men would always be men. She also believed that a woman's job was to be faithful regardless of her husband's infidelity. When I think back on my father's indiscretions, I can say with all honesty that if she had been alive today, she probably would have contracted AIDS from him and died. She was faithful – he wasn't.

My mother wasn't just faithful to her husband. Her faithfulness extended to every area of her life. Not only did she care for ten children, but she also took care of my father's siblings, the people he should have been taking care of as the oldest son and paramount ruler. And then there were all the others too. People would turn up in our village and ask for my mother, and she would take them in, just like that!

It's natural to look back and see the halo we want to see over people's lives. But I know that my mother was a saint. She cared for more than forty people who lived in our compound. This compound consisted of an enclosure in which there was a main house and other smaller houses for members of the extended family and sheds for livestock. My mother was responsible for all who lived there.

How did she provide for them? Well, she was resourceful. In fact, she was a business woman. She used something my father taught her when he returned briefly from the army. He had fallen in love with a fiery drink called *ogogoro* that was sold near the army barracks, and he taught my mother how to brew it. She started her business with one big bottle of ogogoro. But she was so good at brewing it that her customers trusted her more than the other brewers. Soon traders started bringing large barrels to our house for my mother to brew it in. Then they would take it away and sell it in single-glass shots.

Ogogoro is not a drink for the faint-hearted! More often than not, it is brewed to be 100% proof alcohol. To test its potency, people pour it on the floor. If it scorches the floor, they say, "Yes, that's a good one!" So, although my mother brewed it, she never drank it herself, and she didn't encourage any of her children to drink it either. To her, it was a business enterprise, a way to feed her family.

Once, my eight-year-old brother inserted a tube in a barrel in which ogogoro was fermenting and drank it. It was like drinking petrol. His eyes turned white and he fainted. Then he became extremely feverish. My mother wept so hard. She cried out, "God, you know my situation. I have ten children and thirty other mouths to feed. Yes, I brew and sell this spirit. But you know that I have never once tasted it. Neither have my children, until now ..."

That night, it rained. That rain literally saved my brother's life. We carried him outside so that the rain could cool his burning fever and eventually he revived. He never tried to taste the ogogoro again!

Mum told us that the ogogoro was for one thing and one thing only: to generate income so that she could feed us and we could go to school. It was not for us to drink. We saw for ourselves how the money she earned from selling the brew went towards the upkeep of her relatives' children, my father's siblings and us.

Because of her business skills and all the people my mother supported, she was highly respected. People would come to her for advice about family issues. I remember lying in my bed and hearing conversations that continued long into the night. Often, they involved a wife and her absent or non-supportive husband.

My mother would always ask the wife if she had any means of supporting herself. If she said no, my mother would encourage her to start breeding pigs or chickens or begin some business with low start-up costs that would enable her to earn a regular income. That way, she wouldn't have to rely on her husband or her in-laws, and she wouldn't have to endure the shame of going to her family for help. My mother would say, "It's the woman who ends up taking care of the children, so you have to learn to fend for yourself. If you leave your children with your husband, he will marry someone else, and you know what happens to step-children in this village."

My mother used a combination of scare-mongering and sound economic sense to encourage the women to set up income-generating activities for themselves. People still talk about her today in the village and in the family.

Village Life

I have fond memories of growing up in northern Nigeria in a tiny village near Numan town, beside the River Gongola that separates our state, Adamawa, from Benue state. For some reason, our side of the river is dark and brown, while the Benue side of the river is blue.

I had a special friend called Lucky with whom I had many adventures. These included stealing food from our mothers' pantries and trying to discreetly cook and eat it in my or her mother's backyard – as if we could manage that, what with the smoke coming from the firewood!

We also used to rifle through stuff the missionaries in our village threw away, just to find out what we could about these strange people. Once we found some chocolate! As I raised it to my lips, Lucky snatched it from me, and we started arguing. She said the chocolate was hers because she watched out for the missionaries while I was rifling through the bin. I told her that I was the one who suggested the rifling expedition. Moreover, I took the risk by actually rifling through the bin. I threatened to beat Lucky up if she didn't shut her big mouth. In return, she threatened to report me to my mother for stealing. We started scuffling. I'm glad to say that I won and kept the chocolate!

Night times in the village were magical. During the full moon, we would often dance or play *ruwa*, our equivalent of hopscotch. I was the village ruwa champion.

And then there were the village "tea parties". We would collect money from anyone in the village who wanted to contribute. Then we would buy Bongo tea, which I think was made in Uganda or somewhere else in East Africa. When we had enough tea, we would go to the village's big metal drum, put the tea leaves in it, and fill it with water. Then we would boil it. If we could afford it, we would even add a little sugar.

All the villagers would come with their cups, and we give out this Bongo tea. If the villagers wanted to pull out all the stops, someone would provide bread that we would distribute. When everyone had their tea and bread ready, we would all shout, "One, two, three. Say, 'tea party'!" Then we would start drinking the tea.

My brothers had what we called a "record changer", a gramophone. When they started playing music, people would gather round and say,

"Encore! Repeat the music!" and act out the scratching of a needle on a record. Then we would dance.

Yes, village life was hard. But I have some precious memories of village life, too.

Learning to Read

My mother wasn't really educated. I think she stopped going to school at around the age of eight. But she knew education was important. Every day when I came home from school, she would ask, "What did you learn today?" And I would tell her.

Sometimes I made things up, especially when I was just learning to read. I would lie and tell her that we were reading this and that. For example, one of the books I loved had a picture of a python coiled around a Masai hunter. For some reason, this picture fascinated me. I remember asking myself: *What kind of snake is that? So big, coiling itself around something so small!* When I opened the book to that page, I would conjure up a story out of thin air, all the while pretending that I was reading what was written in the book. I guess I wanted to do something for my mother and to take her along with me as far as my imagination could go.

2

GROWING UP

I have always felt different – like I didn't belong anywhere. I know that the circumstances of being born on the side of the road had much to do with this. I saw it as a shameful thing, and I didn't understand why I was the only child out of ten children who had the misfortune to be born in such circumstances. Sometimes to make fun of me, my siblings would call me *Dumne Bishikri*, the name of the market closest to the place on the roadside where I was born.

And why wasn't I given a name by my parents when I was born? Instead, I was named by a nomad, a Fulani man who didn't know anything about me. What if he hadn't given me the name Ladi, meaning Sunday? What then? Would I have carried on being nameless?

My looks didn't help much either. Traditionally, the people of my tribe are dark skinned. However, I was *extremely* dark skinned and was teased relentlessly about my "dark looks". Even my mother – for whatever reason – would say to me, "You are very ugly. You're ugly from inside out. See how dirty, how dark your face is."

I think this was her way of trying to make me strong. She was also trying to help me get over my issues about the circumstances of my birth. I remember sometimes my mother would say, "You are very bad – such a disgrace to me. You are ugly, you're this and that. You're going to kill me." I don't know at the time why she said those things to me. Now, I think it was her way of building my character. But I really didn't handle it well at all.

I began to accept the circumstances of my birth after I became a Christian. I reasoned that Jesus was born in a stable and probably had had to endure insults about his mother's virtue and his paternity all his life, and so I had nothing to complain about. In other words, I learnt to appreciate the story of my birth.

Being Strong

As I was growing up, I was really hard on myself. I did not allow myself to show any weakness, because I thought that was what I needed to do to survive in my village. So I was very determined – even stubborn.

I remember once when I was about ten years old, my mother told me to go and pick up an umbrella from my older sister. She was teaching at a college that was a thirty-minute walk from our home. As I walked home, it started raining. Real African rain, not the gentle rain that falls in other places. African rain pours down like monsoon rain.

I was soaked through. Yet I did not open the umbrella. I passed people who were running for shelter. They asked why I didn't use the umbrella to shelter myself from the battering rain. I ignored them. As far as I was concerned, my mother had told me to bring the umbrella home. She had not given me permission to open it.

When I got home, my mother looked at my small, dripping, muddy ten-year-old body. She stood there in silence.

"But why didn't you use the umbrella?"

"Because you told me to bring back the umbrella. You didn't tell me I could use it," I answered.

My mother burst into tears. "What kind of child are you?" she cried.

That was the problem. I didn't know why I was like that. All I knew was that everything together – my feeling of never belonging; my shame over the circumstances of my birth; my family's constant teasing, "Look at you, so dark!" "Your name is not Ladi. It's Dumna, where you were born!" – gave me a feeling of alienation and disconnection from my family.

I even asked my mother, "Are you sure I wasn't adopted?"

"Of course not, Ladi. What on earth is wrong with you, asking me these kinds of questions? Why can't you just be normal, like your siblings?"

The only way I could manage these feeling was by being stubborn and extremely hard on myself. I thought that if I wasn't weak, people wouldn't take advantage of me.

Village life also had something to do with this attitude. People lived only for the day, and this was reflected in sexual immorality. Children were vulnerable and often molested. By being strong and argumentative, I showed people that I wasn't to be messed with. My best friend, Lucky, said she felt safe with me because I always fought for the two of us. I always stood up for us and made sure we weren't hurt in anyway, in school or at home. I guess that's why my other nickname was "Petrol". Anyone who messed with me was bound to get scorched given the slightest provocation!

But for the Grace of God

As a child, I did have a sense of who God is. I just didn't know him as a Father.

My mother was religious, no doubt about it. She believed in God, but she did not have a saving faith in Jesus. When she heard the bells in the Catholic Church ringing at five in the morning, she would wash her face, cover her head and shoulders with a shawl, and go to church and pray. Sometimes we went with her. At other times she would go and come back, and we would be none the wiser because we were still asleep.

My mother also put the fear of God in us. She would say things like, "If you do what other children are doing, you will be laughed at." This was her way of telling us about the shame of an unplanned pregnancy for unmarried girls. Other times, she would say, "God will not be happy with you." My personal favourite is, "You will not live long if you behave like the immoral girls in the village." It never failed to terrify me, which was her intention all along.

As I mentioned earlier, village life is rather promiscuous. This is partly due to people's ignorance and partly to the philosophy of living for today because you don't know what will happen tomorrow. I could see that my mother was right because I saw for myself what she meant.

The pregnancy of a young, unmarried woman was not celebrated. It was shameful, and girls reasoned that risking a crude termination was better than the shame of having an illegitimate child. So it was not uncommon for us to learn that a girl was pregnant and soon after to hear that she had died at the hands of butchers in the midst of an illegal termination. Many, many young girls died in this way.

This problem was particularly bad during the civil war (1967–1970), when young men were posted all over the region. There were army barracks near our town. The young soldiers had no regard for village girls. They regularly took advantage of them, plying them with alcohol and giving them false promises of the wonderful life they would share together. Once the young men got what they wanted, they would move on to the next girl, leaving their past lover with a broken heart or a pregnancy or both. Some girls were even raped.

With this type of thing going on around me, I had no regard for men. I also feared what my mother would do to me if she found out that I was cavorting with men. (Not that anyone had the courage to approach me – I wasn't beautiful enough and I had a reputation for standing up for myself.)

My mother really didn't want her daughters to experience the same things she had in her marriage with my father. She would always say, "We're happy as we are, aren't we? You don't want some stupid man to turn your head." I agreed, for even as a young girl I was vividly aware of men getting married and then pretty much doing what they liked while their wives struggled.

I saw this in the church too. The services weren't particularly interesting. It was mostly children and women who attended. The men tended to look down on church and even on pastors. They didn't think that the church was a place for real men. So the services consisted of women singing, and the women's groups consisted of women counselling each other about how to handle problems with their husbands. They would tell each other, "Don't leave your husband. He'll marry someone else, and his new wife will ill-treat your children."

Looking back, that is probably where the seed for a women's ministry that educates and empowers women at all levels – financially, emotionally and spiritually – was sown in my heart. I also saw how my mother kept many families together with her wise words and by giving women seed money for little enterprises like pig-rearing or selling fried cassava chips.

But I'm getting ahead of myself.

Meeting Jesus

The most significant thing that happened to me when I was in secondary school was that I met Jesus. Everything I thought I knew about myself changed – forever.

Before this happened, I was a nominal Christian, just like most of the people in our village and many religious Africans today. In other words, I was aware of God, but I didn't have a relationship with him. I didn't know what it meant to be a born-again Christian. I didn't even know what the expression meant!

My mother encouraged us to go to church. She was a committed churchgoer and member of an Apostolic church. When she got married to my father, they moved to Numan, which had a Catholic church that she attended.

I was just over six years old when I started primary school in Numan. When I went to secondary school, I moved to Yola to live with my uncle. I needed to do this because I couldn't travel the fifty-four kilometres (thirty-three miles) from Yola to Numan every day. There I started attending and was confirmed in the Lutheran church, because all my friends went there. Back then, people in my area did not take Catholics seriously because they didn't think they were spiritual enough. I think the Catholic Church just welcomed everyone. It didn't matter to them that their women brewed beer and that members basically did what they wanted, even if they professed a Catholic faith. If people wanted to show their commitment to their religion, they tended to go the Lutheran church because it discouraged drinking and other "evils".

In 1978, I graduated from Government Girls Secondary School in Yola. That was an exciting time. Some companies came to recruit workers from the school. Some girls went off to become airline hostesses – so glamorous! Many others got married, which wasn't unusual. Some of them were even engaged during their secondary school years. I suspect that a good many of them got married simply because there wasn't anything else for them to do.

But I had my life all planned out. I would graduate from secondary school and study law at university. Unfortunately, I didn't get the results I needed to go to university. Instead, I had to go to the College of Preliminary Studies in Yola. This was a pre-university college where you could make up the credits you needed to get admission to university. There I started attending the Fellowship of Christian Students (FCS) meetings in my college. I believe the Western equivalent would be Scripture Union or InterVarsity Fellowship (IVCF). Many Christian leaders in Nigeria today can trace the roots of their Christian life to this fellowship. It was through FCS that I became a Christian in every sense of the word.

It happened at a rally I attended when I was about nineteen years old. I don't know why I went to the rally. I suppose I figured that I had nothing better to do with my time and my friends from FCS would be there. I'm not even sure to this day what I was expecting to find. But I went.

The speaker was Garba Abaga, an evangelist with the Evangelical Church of West Africa (ECWA). He used the *Four Spiritual Laws* booklet, a Campus Crusade booklet that was widely distributed in Nigeria, to talk about the four spiritual laws and about the love of God. He said that Jesus was standing at the door of our hearts and knocking. If I let him come in, he would never leave me nor forsake me.

At that point, everything faded. Tears started coursing down my cheeks. I didn't see anyone or hear anything but what Garba Abaga was saying. I felt like I was the only person in the room. When he said that people who wanted to receive Christ should put their hand up, it was obvious to me that I needed to put my hand up. There must have been at least 1,500 students in that hall. About 300 of those were from my school. But when he asked those of us who had put up our hands to come to the front, I didn't care who saw me. I got up and started walking to the podium.

Campaign workers talked to us and told us to be courageous in sharing our faith. They reassured us that we did not need to be ashamed because we were now born-again Christians. We needed that encouragement for there was a real stigma attached to that label then – as there still is today.

People like to think of born-again Christians as strange people with no joy in life. But every time I felt embarrassed about being a born-again Christian, I remembered what the workers said. Now, it is a label that I wear proudly. But back then, wearing it wasn't easy.

One thing the FCS gave me was a lot of love. Before I joined the fellowship, I didn't feel like I was loved for all the reasons I have talked about earlier. But at the fellowship, I received a lot of encouragement in the Bible study group and in our other activities together.

I was already a disciplined person. But at that fellowship I also learnt how important it is to be rooted in the faith. I learnt how to trust God and believe him and his Word. Most importantly, I learnt to be convinced of his love for me and of his grace upon my life. I really was encouraged by those in the fellowship who constantly told me how well I was doing and how valuable I was in the eyes of God. That kept me going. It still does.

Being Baptized

As a baby, I had been baptized in the Catholic Church in Numan, but now, as a born-again Christian, I was confirmed in the Lutheran church in Yola, which became my home church.

At that time, I chose to change my name to "Gloria", after one of my neighbours from my village whom I was very close to. I wanted to honour her, and the best way I could think of was to take her name. Moreover, the name "Gloria" symbolized what I believed – and still believe – God has to say about me: That my life should glorify his name.

This book is my testimony to what he has been able to do through me.

Teenage friends: Grace Dapwa (now Mrs
Grace Dapwa Agboh) and Gloria Ladi

3

A FATHER TO THE FATHERLESS

I had my life planned out. Marriage wasn't really in the cards, because, to be honest, I felt marriage was something that happened to other women – pretty women. Since I had always been called dark, ugly and stubborn, it seemed highly unlikely that anyone would want to marry me. No, I was going to be a lawyer.

However, things didn't quite work out like that. First, as I said above, I didn't do as well as I should have done at secondary school in order to get the necessary grades to go to university. So I had to spend an extra year or two at the remedial college before I could qualify for university.

Then when I was twenty, my mother fell sick.

My older brother had an important job in the library in Numan and couldn't leave it to take care of our mother. My older sisters were married and had their own families to take care of. One was in Mubi and the other was in Maiduguri, both more than two hundred kilometres from Numan. The other was a teacher and moved around a lot with her four young children. So there was no question about who was going to take care of mother. I was only at college. After taking time off to care for mother, we figured I could simply resume my studies.

So it fell to me to take care of our mother in hospital. Not that I minded. On the contrary, it was a joy, and not because I hated school and wanted to get away. It was a joy because I loved my mother so much.

My mother has passed away, yet she was – and continues to be – an incredible influence on my life. She didn't let my father's desertion steal her compassion. She could have been bitter, but she chose not to be. Instead, she turned her situation around and did good, not only for her children but also for everyone around her – from my father's siblings to the children of relatives she fostered. Now here she was, sick and needing someone to take care of her. What could I have done except go and nurse her? To be able to take care of her was one of the greatest joys and blessings of my life, and a task I took on happily and gratefully.

As soon as I was told that I had to go to her in hospital, I didn't think twice. I packed my things and told my uncle that I was going to my mother. Not once did I even think, "I've not written my exams. I know that I need these exams so that I'll be able to study law at university."

My brother took me to Maiduguri, where he'd had to leave my mother with one of her uncle's wives. We picked her up and went to the teaching hospital.

That hospital was to be my home for the next three months.

Back then, there were no mobile phones or even landline telephones, so there was no way of communicating with people. If you travelled anywhere, people would wait for you to come back. And if you didn't, well ... That was how it was with my mother and me. We did have visitors, and family members came whenever they could. But when they left, it was just me and my mother in the hospital. I suppose that was why I felt that my mother and I were alone in that hospital.

Yes, I did have an older sister in Mubi near Maiduguri. But there was a rift between her and our mother because my mother didn't approve of her marriage. My sister feared our mother's condemnation and so she stayed away from the hospital. This was a shame because our mother had forgiven her and often spoke to me of how she missed my sister. To this day, I don't think my sister has ever forgiven herself for not going to see our mother in hospital. I keep on reassuring her that our mother forgave her before she died. I hope and pray that, in time, my sister will learn to forgive herself.

People often wonder how I can talk about that time in the hospital as one of the most joyous times of my life when my mother was so ill with cancer. I don't know. But I do know that living in that hospital and being with her was one of the most fulfilling times in my life.

My siblings often say that our mother blessed me above all her children because of the way I took care of her in that hospital. In fact, if you ask people who knew me around that time, they would probably say the same thing. But I don't see it that way. All I knew was that I was called to do something that I couldn't wait to do for someone I loved dearly. In that hospital, my mother and I became extraordinarily close. I finally understood her and her love for me. She was so hard on me because she wanted me to be the very best I could be. She wanted me to know myself and not be swayed by the superficial things of the world.

When she screamed at me and called me ugly, it was not because she truly believed that I was ugly. In her own way she was trying to teach me not to rely on my looks to get ahead in life, because beauty – looks – are deceitful. The most important thing is a person's integrity and ambition. I would need those things to get ahead in life, not beauty.

In Christ Alone

African hospitals are not like hospitals in the West. Our culture is familial. It's not unusual to find the relatives of patients living in the hospital with them. Come night time, family members sleep in the corridors, on mats outside the ward, or by the side of their beloved relative.

African culture is also more spiritual than Western culture. The unseen world is as real to us as the physical world, which I think makes us more spiritually sensitive. Prayers are not so much encouraged as expected. That's probably why some wards in Africa look like madhouses, with imams, church ministers and the odd witchdoctor doing their thing with whomever they have come to visit!

My mother was in hospital during Ramadan, the Muslim month of prayer and fasting. So every morning when I heard the muezzin's call to prayer, I would rise from my mat by my mother's hospital bed, pick up my Bible and go out into the corridor where the security light was, to pray. I remember once when I was praying – really praying – big, fat, agonising tears rolled down my cheeks as I begged God to save my mother. Suddenly I heard a voice say, "I love your mother more than you love her."

I looked up and down the corridor and confirmed what I already knew: I was alone. But I knew that I heard something. My heart went cold and my ears red hot. I was so scared I couldn't finish my prayer. I grabbed my Bible and ran back inside the ward to my mother's cubicle.

My mother looked at me and said, "Why are you running?" I didn't know she was already awake.

"Nothing," I said, "no problem, no problem," instead of telling her what really happened.

Later I told my spiritual mentor, Baba Dano, what had happened. He said I should have had the courage to ask God – whose voice was clearly the one that spoke to me in the corridor – to heal my mother. Just like Abraham interceded for the people in Sodom and Gomorrah.

I may not have had my family with me – except my sick mother – but God provided for me in other ways. The nurses really welcomed me into their midst. I don't know what they saw in me. Perhaps they saw a twenty-year-old girl nursing her sick mother. But they really encouraged me emotionally and spiritually. I was able to spend many hours in Bible study and prayer in the nurses' fellowship.

Also, African hospitals being what they are, all kinds of people dropped into the wards all the time. Some of them would come to visit other people and find me there with my mother. They would pray with me and sometimes drop off some money for me. Yes, total strangers would do that! It was how my mother and I survived at the hospital. Back then, the teaching hospital was also free. At least, I don't remember paying anything for my mother's care.

One of the worst experiences I had at the hospital was when my mother had surgery for her liver cancer. When they brought her back to the ward, one of the nurses said that her stitches had to be taken out. So the nurse did that. But when my mother tried to stand, all of a sudden her intestines fell out. I had no time to think. I ran to her, picked up her intestines, put them back inside her stomach, and screamed for a doctor to help me. That was quite possibly the worst day of my life. Nobody should have to do that for anyone, least of all for their mother.

My mother was a strong woman, but after that event, she really struggled. I also think she really didn't want me to suffer so much with her. I was twenty years old, but I was still a child who was seeing and enduring things at the hospital that I really ought not to have done.

The greatest thing that God did for me in that hospital was letting me see my mother come to salvation. One day, when my mother was lying in bed, she had a vision of a man coming into her cubicle. She had never seen him before, so she described him to me when I came. Ten minutes later, the man she had seen in her vision came into the ward and to her cubicle.

He was an old man, and you could see that he was educated. He came to my mother and asked her if she knew Jesus as her Lord and Saviour. My mother responded that yes, she went to church. She didn't speak English, so I translated what the man said in English into Hausa for her. The man said going to church wasn't the same thing. He preached to her, and there before my very eyes, my mother gave her life to Christ.

Then the man disappeared! I couldn't believe it. I ran out to the corridor, but I couldn't find him. I really thought I had seen an angel. But then he came back the next day with his wife to find out how my mother was doing.

I was there when my mother breathed her last. Yes, I was devastated. But I consoled myself with God's promise and what I know to be true: I will see her again in heaven.

When my mother died, the nurses came to clean her up. They brought new bed sheets and wrapped her in them. Two elderly wives of my mother's uncles also came to help clean up my mother and prepare her for burial.

I remember many things from that time. The nurses wrapping my mother's body in the brand-new sheets and moving her gently down the hospital stairs. Men and women from the nurses' fellowship singing church songs as she was being wheeled down. Then, she was loaded on the bus. I got in with my two aunties and started the twelve-hour journey to Yola, where my brother was, with my mother's corpse in the back of the bus.

When she was alive and in the hospital, Mother would say things like, "If I die, do this and that." But I wouldn't hear of it. I would say, "Mama, don't say that. You're not going to die. I will take you back alive to your people at home."

"I don't want my eyes open," she said. "If I die, just do this." She taught me how to pull her eyelids back so they were closed. Then she would smile and laugh.

The chapel at the Theological College of Northern Nigeria (TCNN)

4

SEMINARY

After my mother's death, my father's younger brother got me a job in the accounts department of the ministry of agriculture in Yola. The stories I could tell about that place!

The young people whom I worked with did as they wished. They wouldn't come into work on time – that is if they came in at all! On Saturdays, they came in to do "overtime". They claimed many fraudulent expenses to pad their salaries.

My lifestyle was different from theirs. When they refused to do their work, I would do it for them. It wasn't long before they started calling me "pastor". One day, one of them was reading the newspaper and saw an advertisement for the Theological College of Northern Nigeria (TCNN) in Jos, 400 kilometres (240 miles) from Yola. He said that TCNN would get me out of the department and out of their lives because I didn't belong there, and they were fed up with my Christian lifestyle. "Besides," he said, "A pastor has no business being in a finance department."

"Don't be silly," I told him. "People like me don't go to theological college." I truly did believe that because women weren't ordained in Lutheran or Anglican churches at that time, and I didn't even know that women could do theology.

"Well, if you don't send off for an application form, then I'll do it on your behalf. You are leaving this department. We are fed up with you and your Christian witness!"

I thought he was joking, but he was serious. A week later a response came from TCNN (the Nigerian postal system was good then).

When I saw the form, I sensed a fluttering in my spirit. I can't explain it, other than to say that I felt as if I should go to TCNN. I also considered the practical elements of going to theological college. I would learn new things. With my two credits from remedial college, I could do a diploma in whatever it was I would study at TCNN. For the evangelist diploma, one didn't even need any credits. (I suppose the low entry requirements are one of the reasons people think church ministry is for people who can't do anything else, which I think is a rather unfortunate perception.)

Anyway, we filled in the form together. When we got to the bit where they asked for references, my colleague quickly offered his services. I appreciated his eagerness to sign the form as my referee and consequently get rid of me, but it really wasn't necessary. That honour would go to Reverend "Baba" Danu, my spiritual mentor and a former bishop of the Lutheran Church of Christ in Nigeria.

Baba Danu had a great influence not only on my life but also on the lives of many young students at that time. He helped many in the Fellowship of Christian Students (FCS) who were not from Christian backgrounds by giving them – us – the fatherly care that we needed from a pastor. Incidentally, his eldest daughter, Nahumow was (and still is) a very good friend of mine. When I told her about the TCNN course, she said she was also interested and wouldn't it be great if we could do the course together? So she sent off an application too. We were so silly then ... imagine applying for a course just to keep each other company! But I still smile at those memories.

Baba Danu approved my application form, which I was very happy about. This was in about 1980. At that time, I hadn't even told the uncle I was living with that I was going to theological college. I was making my own plans without his knowledge.

I did the entry exams and came second (although I don't know how many other people took the exams). After that I was called for an interview, which I sailed through. In fact, I was told there and then that I had been admitted into the college.

One of the people who interviewed me was Reverend Alan Chilver, an Englishman. He asked me why I wanted to study theology and what I hoped to do with my qualification. I told him that I believed God was calling me to work with women and young girls.

"Why do you think God is calling you to do this work?" he asked.

I don't know why I said what I did, but looking back, I believe that God put these words in my mouth.

"Because women are not taught in the church nor are they ordained. They just 'do fellowship' – singing songs and all that. But they don't know the Bible. After studying this course, I want to go back to the church and teach the women some theology, so that they can be more knowledgeable about the Bible."

Although I had only been a Christian for a few years, I had a niggling sense that as a woman I was capable of much more than we were "allowed" to do in church. I knew the Bible spoke to both men and women, but I also had questions about the role of women in the church. I've never believed that women can't have an active role besides singing. As far as I was concerned, a Christ-centred life required a thorough grounding in his Word, and every Christian – man or woman – should seek some form of training to better understand how that Word applies to life.

I appreciate gospel music more than anyone. But there is more to Christianity than singing. What good is singing and dancing if you don't have an understanding of the One you profess to follow? How does singing and dancing equip a person, especially a woman, for life?

It also seemed to me that the church really didn't have a role for women, except to sing and cook at church gatherings. This idea was backed up by my experience in the church I attended with my mother as a child and in the Lutheran church where I worshipped as a young believer. The women's idea of fellowship wasn't rooted in theological teaching or the practical application of the Bible to their personal lives. Their understanding of the Bible was traditional. "Fellowship" just meant encouraging each other, usually about "man trouble". Even then, fellowship was telling women not to leave their husbands because "you know what will happen to your children if you leave." What they meant was that after a divorce the children usually remained with the husband and were often mistreated or even thrown out when he took another wife.

I don't know if it was youthful enthusiasm or God who made me give Reverend Chilver such an answer. But what I said is what I actually do now, even though I didn't know what I was saying then.

The government of Adamawa state wanted to encourage women to go to university instead of just leaving school and getting married. So whenever a girl received admission to an institution of higher learning, she automatically received a scholarship. That was the theory. In reality, I only received the scholarship money once because the system was so corrupt. I doubt that some girls ever received theirs at all! But with this partial scholarship and help from my family, I ended up at TCNN, in seminary, to study for a diploma in theology and to meet my future husband, Benjamin Kwashi, who would end up paying my final year's school fees at TCNN.

But, as usual, I'm getting ahead of myself.

Meeting Ben

Being at the seminary was a strange time for me. On the one hand, I was growing as a person and learning all kinds of things about God, the Bible and the Christian life. But, on the other hand, I was still grappling with the emotional and psychological challenge of studying in a city like Jos. To me, it seemed so different from Numan that it could have been England – or at least my idea of what England was like.

I didn't have many friends, but I wasn't worried. In truth, I didn't think that was something one should worry about. Even when I sometimes went out with my friends and their boyfriends and ended up being the third leg, I didn't let that bother me. After a while, I would say something like, "Come on, that's enough. I've got some work to do at home!"

However, I started feeling rather alone, and I wondered why nobody was telling me they loved me. I wondered, *Is it true that I am so ugly?*

Yet I was also determined not to let anyone take advantage of me because of my so-called "village background". Whenever suitors came calling, I frightened them off. I did this despite the fact that deep inside, I sort of wanted to have a boyfriend, someone of my own.

The fact that there were only four women on campus didn't help matters. My friend Anna Rwang was the first woman to be admitted to TCNN. I was the second, although I was the first girl from the Lutheran Church of Christ in Nigeria who went to theological college.

I don't know why TCNN decided to start accepting women. Perhaps they felt it was time. So there I was with my friend Anna, the only other single girl on campus (my friend Nahumow was not offered admission). The other women were all married and lived with their husbands in the married quarters of the campus. Their husbands also attended seminary. Even Anna got engaged and married in due course.

So being at seminary was very tough for me. I wanted to preserve my integrity and dignity, but at the same time, I did want someone of my own, even if I didn't show it. God saw all this and brought me my husband, although the way it all happened was not quite what I expected.

Ben was a year ahead of me in seminary. Anna was in his class and was his very good friend. Because I was the second girl to study at TCNN, it was inevitable that Anna and I would be friends.

On arriving at seminary, I did what came naturally to me and joined the Fellowship of Christian Students (FCS). Ben was the president of the fellowship at that time. I also joined the drama group. I had done drama in secondary school and loved it. Ben was also involved in the group. I joined the singing group, Dynamic Young Ministers. Ben was a member of that group, too.

Ben was very popular. He had a lot of friends and what I thought were girlfriends. I, of course, didn't have a boyfriend. Ben was nice and kind and easy to be around, but he was that way to everybody. I never got a sense that he treated me differently from other people. Sometimes when he was nice to me, my friend Anna would say, "Gloria, be careful. Ben is from Lagos, so he's very sociable. Remember, we are village girls. If a man is being his natural, sociable self with us, we automatically think he is romantically interested in us. So be careful. Remember, he is from Lagos, and you know what those Lagos men are like – very dubious!"

Strictly speaking, Ben wasn't a Lagos boy. He had been born and raised in Jos. However, he had spent some of his youth in Lagos. Back then, Lagos was the capital of Nigeria and our equivalent of New York City. "Lagos boys" were thought to be the devil incarnate – they played fast and loose with unsuspecting women. Anyone who had spent time in Lagos was known as a "Lagos person". So when Anna was warning me off Ben, in essence she was telling me to watch out for the (albeit Christian) smooth talker from Lagos!

I told her he wasn't my type.

When Ben's class was in the classroom next to the library and I passed by, the boys would start shouting. Sometimes they would shout, "Come and see the blackie girl!" Anna, who was in their class, would tell me to ignore them, especially Ben. They were boys, she said, and by nature really quite stupid.

One day, someone sent me a letter and a card with the words, "The miracle of friendship" written on it. I knew who the card was from: one of the leaders of our drama club. I didn't know what he wanted from me, so I told him that I wasn't sure what he wanted. If he was thinking about boyfriend and girlfriend stuff, I told him that he should forget it, because I wasn't interested. In the meantime, I didn't tell anyone about the card, because I didn't want to draw attention to myself. The seminary being what it was, rumours flew around quickly.

You see, I was so focused on achieving what I came to seminary to do that I didn't want to be distracted, even by stupid declarations of love. Coming from a village like I did, I felt it was very important to keep my dignity and not be a pawn in the hands of rich, silly, city boys, like the one who sent me the card. So I didn't tell anyone, not even my friend Anna, about the card. I thank God that I wasn't sexually abused when I was younger, because I know that I wouldn't have told anyone. I was determined to be self-reliant.

The next time I saw the man who had sent me the card was at drama club rehearsal. We had been booked to perform an evangelistic play at the local university. I was the female lead and was really looking forward to performing in front of a live audience the next day. But when we went in for the rehearsal, I saw how arrogant he was, bragging about this and that, when in reality he was nothing as far as I was concerned. It just put me off.

He was supposed to be a committed Christian; he was even in seminary. But there he was being arrogant and generally showing off to me, a village girl. In short, he wasn't showing the Christian qualities one would expect from someone in seminary. Anger burned in me. I didn't want to be around him and let him think that because he sent me a card, I was beholden to him in some way. So I told everyone that I didn't want to take part in the play.

All hell broke loose.

Looking back, I guess I didn't realize how much I would upset everybody by refusing to take part in the play. They pleaded with me to change my mind, but I refused. They tried to get another girl to play my role, but they couldn't. It was the night before our first performance at the University of Jos. After that, we were going to perform at a local teaching college. To say I threw a spanner in the works was an understatement.

Anna pleaded with me to rethink my decision.

I refused.

Ben pleaded with me.

I still refused.

Only God knew the reason for my decision, and I wanted it to remain that way.

After the disastrous rehearsal, I went to the library and then made my way to my hostel. It was about 9:00 p.m. Back then, the single girls lived in the married couple quarters, and the single men lived in the single quarters. The young man decided to follow me from the library. He blocked my way on the path and generally made walking to my hostel difficult. When I confronted him, a torrent of abuse left his lips. He called me a stupid girl. He said that I, a girl from a backwater village, wanted to humiliate him, and if I tried doing such a thing again he would beat me up well and good.

When he left, I stood quietly in the path for a little while. Then I went to my room. My roommate asked me where I had been. I told her not to worry and that I was fine. Then I dropped my books and left the hostel. I knew what I needed to do.

I went to the single quarters where the men lived, stood outside and started shouting.

"I'm going to tell everyone what you did to me! You came to beat me up, and I haven't done anything to you! I want the whole world to know what you're really like, because you're not a Christian. You're a bully and a bad person and everyone should know about this!"

It must have been about 9:30 p.m. at this point. It was a clear night. I made sure to shout at the top of my lungs, so my voice would carry and everyone would hear me. I had to do this because if I didn't, he would have continued to bully me and the trouble wouldn't have stopped. I was a young girl, alone, and I didn't have anyone to fight my battles for me except God. Yes, I came from a village. Yes, I did not come from the city or have rich parents like some of the people in the seminary. But I still had my dignity. If there was one thing village life and my mother had taught me, it was to stand up for myself. Because if I didn't, people would take advantage of me.

So I shouted and continued shouting about how the young man had wronged me by following me from the library to the hostel and threatening to beat me up. People starting opening their windows to see the source of the commotion. Some people came out of the building. The young man didn't know what to do because everyone was asking him what he had done to me. He told them to ignore me. Yet I carried on.

Ben was in his room. When he heard my voice, he shut his window and turned off his lights. I made some more noise and went back to my hostel.

My mind was now at peace.

Ben's Perspective

The drama presentation was a really big deal, and Gloria was a lead actress. I was also acting in the play, albeit in a minor role. Gloria didn't just change her mind about not taking part in the play. She did it the day before our first live audience. We had a script. Everyone taking part had memorized their lines. The university and teaching college had been notified. We had done the publicity for the play. The stage props had been built. Everything was going like clockwork. Then, the day before we were due to perform before our first live audience – at the University of Jos, no less – Gloria said she wasn't going to take part in the play. Nothing we said or did would make her change her mind. Even worse, she didn't give us a reason for her about-face.

I couldn't believe what I was hearing and what she was doing. I may not have been the lead actor or even the president of the drama club. But what she did was really terrible. The whole team was so demoralized. In the end, the events had to be cancelled.

As far as I was concerned, by not taking part in the play, Gloria revealed her true self to everyone – and it wasn't a good thing. She was a village girl, real country-like, strong-willed and with the kind of self-awareness that bordered on arrogance. It was infuriating.

I thought to myself, I am also a prince of my kingdom and the grandson of a king. And not just any king. My great-grandfather abdicated his throne when he became a Christian because he found the traditional beliefs of his tribe incompatible with his new faith. My father was a learned man, one of the first converts of Reverend Miller, a famous Nigerian evangelist in the 1930s. My father had travelled up and down northern Nigeria as an educationalist and reformer. Here was Gloria, putting on airs and graces because she was the granddaughter of the paramount chief of a backwater village. Silly girl!

I was very angry at the rehearsal, so I left straight after the closing prayers. That night, I wrote Gloria two pages of a letter that she will never forget.

I told her how arrogant, proud, stupid and foolish she was.

I told her she was unfit for work in God's kingdom.

I reminded her that she was a backwater princess, because her clan was from Adamawa, a backwater state.

I also reminded her that she was in my territory, where my parents were princes of the kingdom. My grandfather was the king, and my great-grandfather abdicated his throne for the gospel. We were wealthy people. So I wasn't interested in poor, arrogant little princesses with ideas above their station.

Hannatu's second birthday in St Andrew's vicarage, Zaria

5

COURTSHIP AND MARRIAGE

The next day, Ben wrote me a letter. Many of our things have been destroyed in the religious conflicts we have been caught up in after we married, but that letter is the one thing I wish I still had. It was devastating. Ben said I hadn't behaved like a Christian. I refused to take part in the evangelistic drama because I was being selfish. Not content with that, I actually went to the boys' hostel and shamed myself by shouting. The letter ended with this: "Is it because you come from a ruling clan and your grandfather was a paramount chief that you think so highly of yourself? Some of us are more politically and socially connected than you are, and you don't see us making a song and dance about it. Your behaviour was disappointing and not Christ-like."

I didn't know what he was talking about. In the midst of my so-called "plenty" as the granddaughter of a paramount chief, I struggled. I had no one to help me except God. Everything I did was by faith: paying my fees, studying and day-to-day living. I received a small allowance for some part-time work that I did in a local church (the college required students to be attached to a church to learn on the job) and that helped to pay some of my expenses. But in true Nigerian fashion, my scholarship money had been gobbled up by corrupt officials. I certainly wasn't living in the land of plenty.

I was disappointed in Ben. As president of the Fellowship of Christian Students, I thought he would have more compassion. But here he was writing me letters and telling me that I was an uppity upstart from nowhere.

I finished reading the letter and folded it. I didn't tell anyone about it except Anna.

That evening, Ben came to see me. Our living arrangements were simple: my roommate and I had a sitting room and a bedroom with a door between them. When Ben came, I went to the bedroom, picked up the letter and showed it to him. Then I sat down on one of the chairs in the sitting room, arms akimbo, and eyed him balefully.

"Did you write this?" I asked, holding out the letter.

He looked at it as if he had never seen it before.

"Let me have a look," he said.

I waited. I knew what he was doing, and it stirred my anger towards him even more.

Ben looked at the letter and said, "Yes".

"Ben, why would you write such a nasty letter?"

He took a deep breath.

"Because I'm in love with you," he said.

I got up from my seat. "What did you say?"

I was confused. I didn't know what to do. I was going to take back the letter from him. I was going to let him keep it. I was going to …

"Is this love, writing horrible letters to people, telling them how proud and whatnot they are? Is that your version of Christianity? Then, you tell me you're in love with me?!"

As I was talking, I turned my back on him because I was going into the bedroom. I had a vague notion of going to pick up the card and letter I had been sent to show them to Ben so that he could see that my reason for not taking part in the play was not selfish.

The next thing I heard was our front door slamming. I peered through the window and saw Ben running for dear life!

Ben's Courtship

I did not run away. I saw an opportunity to save my life, and I took it!

In my defence, this is what happened.

Very early Saturday morning, 6:00 a.m. actually, someone knocked on the door of my room. I had just finished my devotions.

"Open the door, Ben."

As soon as I heard the voice, I knew it was Anna, Gloria's (and my) friend. I opened the door, and Anna came in and proceeded to abuse me.

"You are a very stupid and crazy Lagos boy! How dare you send such a letter to Gloria! Who do you think you are?!" She went on like that for a while, and I decided to cut in.

"Excuse me, but I don't know what you're talking about."

"What do you mean you don't know?! You wrote such a horrible letter to my friend that she didn't sleep. She was up all night crying!"

"Serves her right," I said.

"Idiot. You made the girl cry and you're happy?"

"I didn't think she was capable of crying," I said. To be fair, I didn't.

"Ben, I'm serious. How could you write something like that to a girl? It's just not done!"

"Fine," I said. "I'll go and see her and apologize."

"Really?"

"Yes, really."

Six months before all of this happened, a very close friend of mine, Obed Dashan, had a private word with me. He said, "Ben, the only woman who can put down the smoke coming out of your head is Gloria. I really think that she will be your wife."

I disagreed with him. "Don't be silly. We're so different. For starters, I'm a fashion addict, and she doesn't have a clue about fashion. And you know what I'm like anyway."

"It is precisely because I know you that I believe she is the girl you need."

I shook my head. "No, I don't need any of these girls. After seminary, I'm just going to go back to Lagos and do my thing."

"No," my friend said. "You won't."

Another of my friends, Jacob, was in the same class as Gloria. He truly believed with all of his heart that Gloria was going to be my wife. I told him, "No way. It can't be."

Then there was a little girl who was the daughter of a married couple, who were students and also Gloria's neighbours on campus. One day, this little girl came running to me and said, "Uncle Benji, when you marry Aunty Gloria, I will be your flower girl!"

"You silly thing," I said.

It would appear that all the signs were there, but I didn't see them. Everyone seemed to have seen that I was going to marry Gloria. Everybody except me, that is.

The strange thing was, for all Gloria's forthrightness and so-called "village ways", she was not short of suitors. Being one of only two single girls on campus definitely had something to do with this. But so did the kind of person she was. For some reason, she attracted the guys on campus like moths to a flame. But they got scorched!

Gloria dispatched her suitors in such a way that it was a miracle that their confidence ever recovered. She would not only reject their advances to their faces. She would go to their hostel, raise her voice and start shouting in such a way that everyone would know she had rebuffed the guy's advances. She did this to at least two guys I knew. As the president of the student fellowship, I once had to tell her that she didn't have to humiliate a guy and decimate his confidence when she turned him down. A plain "no" would have sufficed. That would have been more Christ-like.

Gloria was what we called a "raw creature". What you saw was what you got – no sugar coating. She had never had a boyfriend, so she didn't really know how to behave around men. She came from the village where you had to stand up for yourself if you didn't want people to take advantage of you. So it wasn't surprising that she was like she was. I thought about all this and decided to go and see Gloria in person to apologize.

That Friday evening, I got myself ready to make my apology in person. I had a haircut, shaved, sprayed on aftershave, and put on a brand-new light-blue shirt and good shoes. I had just come back from the UK, so I was not short of things to help my appearance. I also wore a pair of jeans to match. My shoes were leather, so you could hear my steps. Yes, I was going to apologize, but I was also going to intimidate Gloria with my fashion pizzazz.

I went to Gloria's hostel and knocked on the door. What ensued after is now the stuff of legend. But you must understand. Gloria was crazy, and I was the president of the student body. Yes, I came to apologize to her. But I knew what she was capable of. If she started screaming and shouting and calling me names – as she had done to two other guys who had simply professed undying love to her – it would cause a real scandal, and my reputation would be shot to pieces.

When Gloria turned to go into her bedroom, my immediate thoughts were, *This crazy girl is going to come out with a stick to beat me!* So as she went into her bedroom, I opened the front door and ran away for dear life.

I didn't go to my hostel, because I knew Gloria could go there and do whatever craziness was on her mind. She had done that before – I'd seen it. Instead, I went to Obed's hostel, which was the furthest block away from mine and on the edge of the campus. I reasoned that Gloria wouldn't think to find me there. I hung out with my friend, chatting and doing whatnot. Then he told me that he needed to study.

"Well, I am not going to my room," I said. "You can study while I am here."

By this time it was about 1:00 a.m.

"Ben, go to your room."

I told him I wasn't going anywhere. He asked me why.

"I professed undying love to that mad girl, and now I don't know what she'll do," I answered.

My friend laughed.

"Stop laughing! What if she hears you and comes here?!" I said, which made my friend laugh even harder.

"Seriously? She's your wife," he said when he had finished laughing.

I told him he didn't know anything. He said that even though he knew she was mad, he was still convinced that she was my wife.

"Oh well, if she says no, that's fine. I already have my forms to become a monk, so I'll just leave. This is the last straw."

Gloria's Response

Ben really ran! When I saw him through the window, I started laughing. I still don't understand if it was love or whatever that made me laugh. But, I laughed anyway. I might have been a bush girl, but I was also courageous. I didn't have any problems telling people like the guy from the drama group what I thought of him. But Ben was different. He was not like that boy. He was – and still is – someone who once you knew him, you loved him because he had a good heart and was nice to everyone. That was why he was so popular at the seminary. I tried to drum up negative feelings against Ben and find fault with him, but I just couldn't.

When I went to the bedroom, I was going to fetch the letter I had been written by the other guy, I wanted to show it to Ben. Plus, I was still taken aback by Ben's declaration of love.

The next day, Saturday, I sent for Ben. Later he told me he thought I sent for him because I wanted to crow about his declaration. That was why when he came, he thought of many ways to confuse me – like making all kinds of strange requests to completely throw me off balance.

When he arrived, he had paint all over him as he had been helping with some building work on the seminary grounds. I was on the veranda, washing my dishes. When he saw me, he asked me if I had kerosene to get the paint off his hands. I cooked on a kerosene stove, so of course I had kerosene. I gave it to him.

Next, he asked for hot water.

I gave him the hot water.

Then he asked for tea and was just generally erratic. Next thing I knew, he said, "I'll see you later" and left!

After that, Ben would make promises about coming to see me and then wouldn't show up. I found myself liking him, even though we weren't officially dating or anything. Then I didn't like seeing him because I got confused every time he was around. If I was in the library, he would ask me what I was reading, and I would tell him that I didn't know – because I didn't.

Sometimes, Ben would come and visit me with his friends, and I would lock myself in my bedroom and refuse to come out until everybody left. The reason was partly because of my village mentality. I didn't want anyone accusing me of entertaining men in my room. But at the same time, I honestly didn't know how to be sociable and entertain people. Believe it or not, I was also shy. So it was easier to hide in my bedroom. Eventually I told my friend Anna what was happening, and she told me not to rush. "Remember, he's a Lagos boy. Girls like him. So beware!"

Yes, Ben was by nature a sociable person. I have always said that he is the only person who can really make me laugh, and I really needed to laugh more because I was so focused and serious-minded. However, as I got to know Ben better, I discovered his serious side. I was also praying with some of my friends about this stuff. But I knew that I was comfortable with Ben.

Eventually, Ben and I started dating. But we had no end of problems because he didn't understand why I was the way I was. He is fun to be around, expressive and just generally a nice person. I was stubborn and determined not to let anyone take advantage of me and so serious about everything. I just didn't know how to let my guard down.

I suppose that's why he found it hurtful that I didn't respond to any of his letters when he graduated. I'm not an expressive person like he is. I know it sounds unbelievable, but when I received his letters, I just didn't know what to do. Ben is articulate and affectionate, and in the course of our married life, I have really learnt to relax and not be so serious all the time. But back then, that behaviour was alien to me. What made it worse was that I genuinely didn't know how hurtful people found my actions. Like they say, we live and learn!

Ben's Proposal

I finally asked Gloria whether she would marry me.

She didn't answer. But she didn't say no either. I knew how shy she was and the enormous self-respect she had, so I didn't push her. I was preparing for my graduation and ordination and didn't want to rock the boat. So I left things as they were. However, Gloria was there at my ordination. Then I went as a single priest to Wusasa, Zaria, about 300 kilometres (186 miles) north of Jos, to start my life in the mission field.

I didn't hear from Gloria.

This was in 1982, before there were mobile phones, email, text messages, Facebook or anything like that. I couldn't contact Gloria by telephone because there weren't any for the students in seminary. Only in exceptional circumstances could students use the principal's landline and a heartsick priest hardly counted as an emergency. I became very concerned and sent Gloria cards (twenty of them).

No response.

I wrote Gloria more than fifteen letters.

She didn't reply to any of them.

I was troubled. I couldn't go to her graduation because I was in the parish and couldn't have time off. Being a single priest in Zaria was – not to put a fine point on it – delicate.

Things were going really well for me in Zaria. God really blessed my church members and my ministry in my first year. The Bishop of Kaduna was overjoyed with all the things I was doing in the church and kept on encouraging me. My archdeacon loved me. My chairman loved me. The women loved me. Everybody loved me and was happy with me. Everybody except me. I was heartsick and miserable. Gloria still hadn't replied to my messages. I had to take drastic action.

On 23 September 1982, which was also my birthday, I knelt by my bed and prayed: "Lord, please give me a wife. You know my calling. I want to serve you. I don't want to fail you. I want to raise children for you. I don't want to give any credence to the stories of pastors' children being horrible. Mine will not be. Lord, please give me a woman who will help raise godly children."

I took out a list with three names on it. I pointed to the first name on the list, and I heard a voice clearly say within my spirit and also reverberate around the room: "That's not your wife."

"What about this one? She's a nurse."

"That is not your wife," the Voice said.

My heart was in my mouth. I couldn't mention the third one. Yet I knew I had my answer. By this time, it was 10:30 at night and I was dressed for bed. I went to the bathroom, packed my toiletries in an overnight bag, put on my jeans and a shirt and went outside where my car, a brand-new little panel van, was parked. I threw the overnight bag in the back of the van and hit the road.

I filled up the tank and drove through the night. I know that I was speeding. But nobody was on the roads. Just me and some goats and ducks on some of the streets. As I came up Jengre hill, smoke blinded my vision. When it cleared, I found myself facing a Coca-Cola truck coming up the hill from the opposite direction. I slammed my brakes hard and went into the bush on the right to avoid hitting the truck. If I hadn't done so, I would have gone underneath the truck, a dead man.

By 8:00 a.m., I reached Numan. The whole journey had taken nine hours. I went to see Gloria who was staying with her older sister. When she saw me, Gloria, typical Gloria, did not say "Good morning", but instead said, "What brings you?"

My heart sank. This was Saturday morning. On Friday, I had finished choir practice and gone straight back to my little priest house to pray. No one in Zaria had any idea where I was. If I had died on Jengre hill, crushed by the Coca-Cola truck, my disappearance would have been a mystery that only heaven could have revealed. I let Gloria's words wash over me. I had made it safely to Numan. That was the important thing, so I reminded myself to focus on that.

I had a bath and was given breakfast. Gloria went to call her older sister.

"Ben is here," she called out. My eyebrows shot up. I thought, So, Gloria had told people about me. She must have feelings for me. She just chose not to show them or reply to my letters.

Her family came downstairs. I was given a nice welcome, which surprised me. But inwardly I said, "Thank you Lord, thank you Lord. I think I definitely have my answer now."

After breakfast, Gloria asked me to take her some place. I thought this was strange, but continued to play along. She jumped in the van and directed me to her auntie's place. Once again, everyone was nice to me. Then Gloria took me to her grandparent's house and the same thing happened. Then we went to see her father. Finally, I got it: Gloria was showing me off.

We came back to her older sister's place in the evening. "Tomorrow we will finish it," she said.

I told Gloria I was leaving that night because the next day was Sunday and no one knew where I was.

She didn't believe me. She got really angry. Her eyes flashed and she started crying. I placated her, and eventually she believed me. At 10:00 p.m., I got in my van and drove back to Zaria. By 9:00 a.m. the next day, I was preaching in my church, and my congregation was none the wiser about the events in the life of their pastor over the last twenty-four hours. But, that was fine with me. I had received my answer: Gloria had said yes. Finally, I was at peace.

Engagement and Wedding

I didn't really have much to do with Ben's formal proposal. He sent his friends to put out feelers about the possibility of my marrying him and I made it known – in my own shy way – that I was open to it. I also told them how things were done in my village, with the dowry and all that. Ben's friends took note and reported back to Ben. In all fairness, I wasn't really involved in our engagement because that was how we did things. The fiancée was kept in the background while the families did the negotiating and introductions.

Having said all that, I know what happened when Ben went to see my father in Numan, because my father called me. He wanted to know if I was okay with the engagement. I said "Yes". Ben laid out the dowry and that was it: we were formally engaged.

Trouble was, I was clueless about how to organize a wedding. I had only the vaguest idea of what would be involved. All I knew was that the bride should wear a wedding gown. So Ben and his sisters ended up planning the wedding and everything. But they were great.

They would bring things for me to approve, and I would say, "Anything you choose and do is fine with me." It wasn't that I wasn't interested. Far from it! I was ignorant about such things! I just didn't know what to do.

As we were planning the wedding, Ben asked me about the friends I was inviting. I told him I didn't have any, and I didn't. Most of my friends were my relations. My perception of getting married in the Anglican Church was that the bridesmaids had to be unmarried, which further narrowed down the pool of available candidates. In the end, I chose my school classmates as bridesmaids and friends of the bride.

As for marriage, well, I was clueless about that as well. I thought marriage simply meant living with a man, cooking for him, having children and keeping the house clean. Perhaps if I had married someone else, that would have been my life. But my idea of marriage then and what God had in store for my life were two completely different things.

6

A GROWING SHADOW

I graduated from TCNN in June 1983. In December I got married and moved to join Ben at St Andrews Church in Wusasa, Zaria, about 300 kilometres (186 miles) north of Jos. My assumption was that I would live the traditional life of a woman married to a pastor who is an evangelist through and through. You see, Ben's never happier than when he's in a remote bush village somewhere preaching Christ to people like the Isawa, the Jesus People, who were also Muslim. Ben regularly went into the bush to minister to these people. Yes, he was a pastor, but in his heart of hearts, he's an evangelist. So I thought that I would spend my life supporting my husband, a simple bush evangelist, and bringing up our children in the Christian faith, making sure that they were free from the curse of being the "pastor's children".

But once again God had other plans.

Life in Zaria

Even before I got to Wusasa, I already had a job. In September, Ben had told his bishop, Bishop Ogbonyomi, that his fiancée had also studied theology. The bishop was so excited that he asked to see my diploma. And that was how I started lecturing at St Francis of Assisi College in Zaria. I taught Old Testament, theology, ethics and African traditional religions. I also taught Hausa certificate courses and diploma classes.

If anyone had told me that I would end up teaching at that college, I would have laughed in their face. But I did, and that I did is a testament to God's grace upon my life. I didn't think people like me did things like this: lecture on theology and ethics and eventually become the wife of a bishop. But I think of my name, Gloria, and what it means to me as a Christian – that my life should reflect God's glory and grace in everything I do. Then I'm really thankful to the Lord for being so gracious to me.

But the fact that I was lecturing did not mean that I was not also a pastor's wife. I became increasingly aware that when Anglican men went into ministry, they had theological training, but their wives had none. Yet their wives were expected to lead the women and to take on other leadership roles in the church, despite often being ill-equipped for the task.

So I approached Bishop Ogbonyomi for permission to start a women's theological training school at St Francis of Assisi College. More precisely, I told him that I wasn't leaving his house until he did something about training women in the church.

"But the Anglican Church does not ordain women," he said.

"All the more reason you should set up training courses for them. I am more fortunate than most pastors' wives because I went to a theological college. How can you expect other pastors' wives to take up the spiritual responsibility of leading the women and children of the church if they haven't got a clue about the fundamentals of theology, much less the harsh realities of being a pastor's wife? Even if all you can give these wives is six weeks' training, then do it. It is necessary."

Bishop Ogbonyomi – bless him – said, "Okay Gloria. Have your way. Just remember, I haven't got the budget for this!"

"I don't need your money. I will raise it."

And I did. I'm a firm believer that if something needs to be done to the glory of God, then he will find a way. All I wanted was the go-ahead from the bishop. Once I had that, I told the church women and we started fundraising. That was how we raised the funds and established the women's department at the St Francis of Assisi Theological College in Zaria.

We even wrote letters to churches asking for food supplies so that the women who came would have something to eat. I think they are still doing that today. The women's theological training school is now a big department at St Francis of Assisi, and I started it. Imagine that!

I still start women's programmes wherever I go. Not just for the sake of it, but where they are needed. As an African woman, I know how important it is to be encouraged and empowered. I'm not just talking about economic empowerment, although that is important too. For the most part, I'm talking about education, because I believe that education empowers women. I am fortunate to have a husband who believes in this and supports me.

Ben served in Zaria from 1982 to 1987. By the time we left, he was also the leader of the Zaria chapter of the Christian Association of Nigeria (CAN). That meant he was the leader of all the Christians in that region. It was a huge responsibility and one Ben took seriously. His father was a highly educated man, and Ben had learnt much from him about Christianity in Northern Nigeria and about the social and political problems in the region. So Ben had a lot of political information that I didn't have a clue about. And he talked about it.

Ben is outgoing and has such a vibrant personality that when he speaks, people listen. So when he starts talking about the history of Christianity in Northern Nigeria and the secret deals that were made between certain political figures, from colonial times to now, to marginalize and eventually neutralize Christianity there, people get nervous. They can't dispute his facts, because Ben is a man of papers who has dates and documents to support what he says. But they can attack him.

So when Ben started talking about these things, I would get scared – I was rather timid then – and ask him why he was raising all these questions about the persecution of Christians in northern Nigeria. Visitors would come to our house, and they would talk through the night. Other times, they would go to all-night prayer meetings and come back praying, "God help us. The evil plans of the enemies of Christianity will not succeed."

When political appointments were made, Ben would research and ask critical questions about the process of appointment. In the pulpit, he would preach and challenge the appointees to stand up and show their Christian faith – the Christian appointees, that is. He would also challenge them to be different from the corrupt leaders we had.

At the same time, Ben also worked with university professors doing research on what some Muslims were trying to do in northern Nigeria.

He is a thorough person and wanted to draw attention to what was happening. But it seemed nobody was listening.

In the midst of a period of ethnic religious conflict in Zaria, I remember Ben preaching a sermon that I will never forget. His text was Exodus 14:13: "Do not be afraid. Stand firm and you will see the deliverance the Lord will bring you today." He urged Christians to stand firm in the knowledge that God will fight our battles for us. All we have to do is stand strong. Ben was passionate and strong in his beliefs.

This was in the early 1980s. Now when we listen to the recorded tapes from those days, I ask him how he knew about these things. He says that he found them all while reading the Bible. Because Ben was so vocal, he became a target and plans were put in place to have him eliminated. But the Anglican Church had its own security for him, and he was regularly hidden away for his own safety.

Looming Troubles – Ben's Perspective

I was in seminary when Ayatollah Khomeini successfully overthrew the Shah of Iran. I don't know why, but I took note of the celebrations around the Muslim world when the news was announced. Soon after that some people in northern Nigeria began to talk openly about Usman dan Fodio, a Fulani who led a jihad in 1804. The more I heard about him, the more my interest was piqued.

Around this time, there was a man in Durban, South Africa, called Sheikh Ahmad Deedat. He was an Islamic theologian who devised a theological approach that was unique at that time. He would use the same methods that we Christians used – public preaching and apologetics – to tear the tenets of the Christian faith to shreds. For example, he would say that Jesus is not the Son of God and dispute the theology of original sin. Sometimes he would challenge Christians to drink poison because Mark 16:18 says that Christian will drink poison and not die. So if Christians really believe the Bible, they should be able to drink poison and be confident that they will not die.

In 1980, Josh McDowell, the famous American Bible teacher and apologist, took on Ahmad Deedat at a public debate in South Africa on the resurrection. I couldn't go because the apartheid policies of South Africa meant that they weren't granting visas to Nigerians. (The Nigerian government, too, banned all contact with South Africa.) They had a fantastic debate, and McDowell did really well, I believe. But that wasn't the end of it. At some point after this debate, Ahmad Deedat suddenly became very popular in Nigeria. A movement began to resurrect the 1804 jihad that had conquered much of northern Nigeria.

Initially, Ahmad Deedat's theological puncturing of the Christian faith didn't raise any concerns because it wasn't violent. But by 1981, specific movements began to take shape. A large group of educated young men emerged out of mainstream Islam and started calling for an Islamic state in northern Nigeria where I was born, lived and worked. Some people in the government began to take note of this movement. But we were under military rule then, and the government as a whole did not want to take any action that could "touch religion".

Then in 1987, a Christian preacher named Abubakar Bako was accused of misquoting the Qur'an while speaking at the Kafanchan College of Education in Northern Nigeria. I'm sure that his sermon was recorded, but nobody bothered to listen to the tapes to see if the allegations were true. Instead, riots broke out and for the next three days there was a systematic cleansing of Christians in Kafanchan. The number of Christians there was sufficiently large for them to be able to defend themselves to some extent, but things were a lot worse when the unrest travelled the 178 kilometres (110 miles) from Kafanchan to Zaria where we were based. In Zaria, Muslims were in the majority, and Christians had a much harder time.

The military government sided with the Muslims. The president, General Ibrahim Babangida, declared Abubakar Bako a wanted man. The northern leaders pronounced a fatwa against him that called for him to be killed. Yet Bako had not been formally charged and had no opportunity to face his accusers in court.

Those events marked the beginning of the military government's bias against Christian minorities in northern Nigeria.

While all this was going on, I was a young pastor with a young family. I was also a Nigerian, and a Northerner. I thought I was helping my northern people by establishing schools and clinics. I thought I was providing education for everyone because where I grew up and worked, we had always lived together as Christians and Muslims without any distinctions. We were doing community development, which was something the military government woefully failed to do for the people.

The leaders were asking Nigerians to be patriotic. But this same military regime was unable to protect me when my house and church and the houses of the Christian community were torched and we needed their help. They were unable to protect a Nigerian who was a Northerner and also a Christian. That bothered me.

I used to be puzzled as to why the military government reacted as it did. But I think that now I understand its thinking. It was afraid of any populist movement or any possibility of an uprising against them. They were also afraid of Christians because they didn't understand the Christian message. The message is a populist one – it is the truth, so people follow it. But it is never a truth against the government simply for the sake of being critical. Rather, the gospel enlightens, sets captives free, opens the eyes of the blind and empowers its leaders to be the voice of the voiceless and defenders of the poor, widows and orphans. Inevitably this brings confrontation between Christian leaders and corrupt, dictatorial, oppressive and insensitive governments. No Christian preaching is ever against a government but it is against injustice, insecurity, lack of equal opportunities and unfair and inequitable distribution of national wealth. Even the father of liberation theology, Gustavo Gutierrez, who opposed the injustice of governments did not start uprisings against them.

But our military government did not know any better. The kind of preaching I was doing was enlightening the minds of people. It was opening their eyes to what was going on in their communities and to corrupt practices in government. So I was seen as a threat. Unfortunately for me, the military government was led by a Muslim.

And what was I preaching? I grew up in a Nigeria where my father, a Christian, walked with Ahmadu Bello, the Sardauna of Sokoto, a well-known and popular northern Muslim leader. I also grew up in a compound where my father, mother and older sisters, all devout Christians, supported Bello and were unapologetic about it. I grew to love Aminu Kano, another northern Muslim politician, more than Bello.

I love poor people, and I love to see their good. I grew up in a Nigeria where we had constant electricity until we had a military government under Ibrahim Babangida. Then our standard of living began to fall, drastically. When I preached about these things, I was preaching against what was happening to Nigeria because the country was going backwards. I come from a military background, yes. But I was opposed to military rule because it wasn't doing us good. I was advocating change.

After our home in Zaria was burnt down, I realized that my safety could not be guaranteed. But I had to keep crying out on my own behalf and on behalf of all those who had died voiceless. The intolerance towards Christians was strong, but it was hidden. It would come out in bursts and sparks when we had a "crisis". But back then, we had no press with cameras everywhere like we have today. Many atrocities were committed against Christians in 1987, and they continue to the present day.

The Muslim-dominated military government didn't know how to handle the situation. But they wanted to stay in power. So if the "rascally Muslims" killed the "noisy Christians" to silence them, so much the better for their chances in political office. In short, the government at that time was building a systematic theology of hate in the country that has bedevilled northern Nigeria to the present day. It would seem that little by little, the military government surrendered power to the so-called "rascally Muslims". They would make noises about investigating atrocities, but nothing was ever done.

Fire in Zaria

The three-day orgy of killing in Kafanchan as the Muslims sought to redress what they felt was an affront to their religion soon spread to Zaria where we lived. Something happened that lit a spark at the University of Zaria's campus, and trouble spread through the city like wildfire. Muslims and Christians were at war with each other.

I wasn't in Zaria at the time. My uncle had died, and I had travelled down to Numan with my youngest son, Rinji, leaving my two-year old daughter Hannatu at home with Ben. I remember exactly what I was doing when someone came in and told me that they had just come from a fellowship meeting where they had prayed for the Christians in Zaria and for the Christian leader there who had been killed. I was trying to pour hot water into some baby food to feed Rinji. I stood there. The water poured into the floor, and I didn't even notice.

All I could learn was that there was a religious crisis and that the leader of the Christians in Zaria had been stoned to death. My husband was the president of the Zaria chapter of the Christian Association of Nigeria. That made him the leader of the Christians in Zaria. The leader was said to have been a short man from Jos in the Plateau State. They said he was preaching and somebody threw a stone at him. He fell and pandemonium broke out. Well, Ben was short, and he was from Plateau State. As for him being stoned while he was preaching, I wasn't really surprised. My husband is a man of conviction. Whenever he preaches, people react in one of two ways: they are either challenged or affronted. It is always one or the other.

I thought about the death of Stephen the martyr in the Bible. I thought, *That was how Ben died*, but I didn't want to believe it. My body started shaking. I didn't know what to do with myself. So I stood there with the hot water pouring on the floor, and my six-month-old son clutching my ankles.

I recalled one of the sermons Ben had preached to thousands of people a few weeks before. He was so young, but he had authority. He preached on Exodus 14, crossing the Red Sea. He urged the Christians to look ahead. The previous year (1986) the military president Ibrahim Babangida had signed up Nigeria to what is now known as the Organization of Islamic Cooperation, thus declaring it a Muslim country. Ben had voiced his concerns about this action, for in terms of its constitution Nigeria is neither a Muslim nor a Christian country, but a secular one.

When he preached that sermon, there were already rumblings of trouble in Zaria. There had been one or two incidents when Christians had been slaughtered, and some Christians wanted to take revenge. But Ben cautioned them against it and told them that God would fight for them.

He was so young when he preached that message. I didn't know much about all these "big" things, busy as I was with our two young children. But as I stood in the kitchen that day, reeling from the news that my husband had been stoned to death, I remembered the words of that sermon: "Heaven and earth will pass away, but my word will remain forever. Stand firm! God will fight for you. Heaven and earth will pass away, but the Word of the Lord will stand. Stand firm, children of God. He will fight for you! Vengeance is his. Stand firm!"

Those words kept reverberating in my head: "Heaven and earth will pass away, but my Word will remain forever. Stand firm!"

I physically and mentally shook myself. I had to go and see for myself what was left of my home and find out what had happened to my husband and daughter. I made the trip back to Zaria in a zombie-like state. When I got there, some women from my church took me to our house.

I couldn't believe what I saw. The roof had been blown off. There was nothing, absolutely nothing left of our home – it was just ashes. I think the women thought that I would start crying. They didn't know that God had already comforted me through Ben's sermon that had been reverberating in my head from the minute that I heard he had been killed. God reassured me through that sermon that heaven and earth will indeed pass away, and if persecution and hardship did not start with the leaders of his church, who would believe the stories of the congregation?

As I looked at the ashes of our house, all I could hear was my husband's voice: "Heaven and earth will pass away, but God's Word will remain." I looked at the ashes and thought, Yes, it's true. Heaven and earth will pass away. It is only God's Word that stands.

While I was in Numan, Ben had a premonition that trouble was coming. He had spent some time praying with Bitrus Gani, one of the leaders of the church. Concerned about the reports he had heard on what was happening in Kafanchan and about one or two incidents in Zaria, he went to the police. They assured him that all was well and that the Christians in Zaria had nothing to fear.

But the very next day, a security agent came to Ben and warned him of a plan to kill all the key leaders of the church in Zaria. Because Ben was vocal on many issues, he would definitely be targeted. The agent said that if Ben was killed, the crisis would become even greater. So he begged Ben to leave our house because the murderers were coming that night.

Initially, Ben didn't believe him. But some members of our church who were also in the army persuaded him and Bitrus to leave their houses and go to a safe house. That was how their lives were spared. That night, our houses were attacked. They also burnt the church – razed it completely. Absolutely nothing was left except ashes.

By the following day, over one hundred church buildings and over three hundred homes had been burnt down.

Eventually Ben managed to track us down, and we stood looking at the ashes of our first home. All I had was a wrapper (a length of cloth tied around the chest). Rinji had a pair of jeans and a t-shirt. Hannatu had just a dress. Ben had a t-shirt and a pair of trousers. That was all we had – the clothes on our backs – and nothing else.

The Bishop of Kaduna immediately arranged for us to be transferred from Zaria to Zonkwa, 260 kilometres (160 miles) to the south. Ben took some of the ashes of our Zaria home with us as a reminder that we were living on borrowed time.

I wouldn't say that after this event he was more careful, for he still speaks out today.

7

INTO THE MISSION FIELD

When I think of the events of the next few years, I think of the difficulties of the mission field.

Zonkwa

Back in 1987, the people of Zonkwa weren't as educated as they are today. They had never had a pastor who owned a car. In fact, the richest person in the village owned a motorcycle. So when we showed up in my husband's panel van, the villagers took an instant dislike to us. They accused us of showing off and thinking we were better than they were, even though we had lost everything to arson in Zaria.

I like to be active and of use. So one of the first things I did when we arrived in Zonkwa was to set up a fellowship for girls in the village. I told everyone about my intention. My house wasn't far from the church hall, so I went there to remind the girls that our first fellowship meeting would be beginning soon and that I didn't want them to be late. I was hanging around in the back of the hall when I heard voices. The mother of one of the girls was bad-mouthing my husband to the other women there. They didn't realize I was there, or if they did they did not know that it was my husband they were bad-mouthing. So they gave free rein to their tongues.

The village women called Ben a radical. They said that because he was from Lagos, he had come to show off his "big" van and sleep with their daughters. They said that I was no better. Who did I think I was coming to teach their children and start a "ministry" for girls? They would do their "ministry" themselves, they said. They didn't appreciate people like me and my husband telling them what to do.

I stood and listened. I looked really young then, so they didn't realize I was Ben's wife. These were people who weren't trained in children's ministry. By the time their girls reached the age of twelve or thirteen, most were pregnant. Sometimes they even had sex on the main road. I knew that because I had seen it myself. I burned with anger and thought, *How dare they?! Did they even know how much we had suffered and sacrificed, only to end up in this god-forsaken place where people had no morals and sense of decorum?!*

One of the women told the girls to go home and not bother about the girls' fellowship. She said it was "nonsense". I walked forward from where I had been standing near the girls and went up to the women.

"Well, they are your daughters, so you can do what you want with them. But I just want you to know that my husband hasn't slept with any of your daughters. I love these girls like my own. But to each her own."

One of the women almost fainted. The others started protesting. I ignored them and told the girls that they were free to come back in the evening for their fellowship if they wanted.

Ben with Hannatu and Gloria with Rinji outside their home in Zonkwa

We were in Zonkwa for about a year. With God's grace, we managed to accomplish much. I believe wholeheartedly that our best came out in that place in that one year.

Kaduna

We left Zonkwa when the bishop transferred us to Kaduna Polytechnic. Ben was supposed to be the first chaplain there, but as you can probably guess, it didn't quite work out like that.

We had – not to put too fine a point on it – an interesting time at the polytechnic. There wasn't any accommodation for us, so we were given a room right next to the hall of the Catholic social centre, where there were regular parties, receptions and other social events. Where there is food, there are rats. Not cute little Western rats, but huge African rats the size of small dogs. They were as crafty and vicious as they were huge.

It was horrible, horrible, *horrible*. I still shudder just thinking about it.

The worst shock involved our few belongings. After our house burnt down in Zaria, we had nothing except the clothes on our backs and had started again from scratch. The church in Zaria had kindly given us some things when we moved to Zonkwa. That was still all we had. Village life – as anyone will testify – is not easy. We were a young family of four living on the pittance of a priest salary. I'm not complaining – I'm just saying that was the way things were.

When we moved to Kaduna, we packed these goods into cardboard boxes and sent them on ahead. They were taken to our room before we arrived. So once we had got the children settled, we opened one of the cardboard boxes. We couldn't believe our eyes. Everything we had been given was gone! The little t-shirts for our children, the new shoes ... the rats had eaten everything!

We opened the next box, and the rats had got to that one, too. And the next box, and the next. It was all too much. Ben and I just started crying. First the Muslims burnt our house. Then we went to Zonkwa, a place of heathens, to do the Lord's work and got nothing but hassle from the villagers. And now in Kaduna, no arrangements had been made to accommodate our young family. We were expected to provide spiritual counsel to students, and here we were living in a room attached to a community centre that was overrun with apocalyptic rats. We wept.

Somehow we managed to pull ourselves together – as one does. There was too much work to be done to dwell in self-pity. But it was tough. Sometimes when we were sleeping, we would hear the rats in the ceiling, or just running around. They would drag something, and if it fell and woke us up, they would be still. It was horrid!

In the meantime, my husband was fighting his own battles with the polytechnic about his chaplaincy. We had been told that a student chaplaincy was available. But when we arrived, there was no chapel. What Ben found instead was lots of resistance to his chaplaincy. I really don't know what it is about my husband, but everywhere we went, trouble followed him, and us ...

When Ben reported for work, he was told that some funds had been put aside by the founders of the polytechnic for a chapel on campus. However, for reasons that we could never quite figure out, the chapel had never been built. When no answers were forthcoming, Ben – as he was wont to do – took matters into his own hands and decided to build the chapel himself, with his bare hands.

He selected the location of the new chapel – by the gates of the polytechnic – and started publicising his building plans. In the two months that we had been there, he had been able to raise funds to build the chapel. My husband is a determined man, and when it comes to preaching the gospel, he will do whatever is necessary to get the Word out.

Suddenly, Ben was summoned by the rector and told to shelve his building plans because the chapel would cause "problems" on campus. We didn't know it, but some Muslim students had been threatening repercussions if it was built.

Ben is not easily intimidated. He has strong views about his calling as a preacher. With the events of Zaria still fresh in his mind, he believed that we were living on borrowed time. The urgency of doing God's work in the limited time we had left was still ringing in his ears. So he didn't take the threats seriously. As far as he was concerned, he had been called to do a very important job in the lives of the students, and he was going to do it – threat or no threat. Was he going to run from Muslims or any other threat all his life?

Ben started marking out the foundations of the chapel. Then he called for students to come and start digging. Tensions rose on the campus, but still Ben and the students continued digging.

The following week, the school closed down. The authorities were worried. There was tension between the Christian students who were building the chapel and the Muslim students who were threatening to burn it down. Ben, ever pragmatic, said, "Fine. Since the school is now closed, technically, there is no security situation. I'll stay on site, and any student who is still interested in building the chapel should come. Masons, carpenters ... this is a polytechnic! Come one, come all. Let's build the chapel."

While all this was going on, our bishop was also wrestling with the fact that Ben hadn't completed his bachelor's degree in divinity. He had a diploma in theology, but not a bachelor's degree. So after four months at Kaduna Polytechnic, we were bundled away and taken back to the Theological College of Northern Nigeria (TCNN), Jos, where we had met and got married.

I was asked to go back to Zaria to continue lecturing, while Ben studied at Jos. But I didn't think it was right for me to be away from my family. My place was with them. I didn't really care what I did – cook, clean, whatever – as long as we were together. So I went to TCNN with my husband.

Initially, I thought I would just do the diploma in divinity. But I was tested and told I could do the bachelor's degree in divinity as well. So I joined my husband's class, and we graduated in the same year.

TCNN, Jos

We had a wonderful time at TCNN. We were there for two years, and it was so peaceful. Ben used to joke during our time there that he had never realized that life could be so peaceful!

Ben was still misunderstood: some people thought he was too outgoing and a show-off. But we had very good friends who supported us. As usual, Ben took part in everything. He helped to build the library ... he made himself available as unofficial chaplain ... he mowed the grass

... he was just busy! But I didn't complain. I was grateful to get some peace and quiet after all the upheaval of the last few years.

Back to Zaria

After earning our bachelors' degrees in divinity at TCNN, our lives took an unexpected turn. We were asked to go back to St Francis of Assisi Theological College in Wusasa, Zaria, where I had taught before.

This time Ben was to be the principal, which he was really happy about. I was happy as well because I thought that being surrounded by his beloved books and intellectual debate would keep Ben out of trouble. Being an academic gives one some immunity. Ben could confer, criticize and debate at will with bishops from the inside out and could speak as an academic authority and evangelist. Most importantly, he would be listened to and not lynched.

I was also excited that I would now have an opportunity to firm up the women's department that I had established a few years earlier. I was going to train and teach women theology, Bible studies and the practicalities of a life in ministry. Our two years' studying at TCNN had been great, and I wanted to extend that period of peace for as long as possible. Being at St Francis was certainly going to provide that peace for us.

Finally, we were settled as a family. Or so I thought.

The Offer

Towards the end of our time at TCNN we had met Robert (Bob) A. Kolb, Professor of Pastoral Theology at Luther Northwestern Theological Seminary in Minnesota, USA. He was on a sabbatical in Jos and heard Ben preach. After the service, he went up to Ben and asked him who I was.

Ben has a tendency to talk about me in his sermons. He often says that he cannot preach a sermon without making some kind of reference to me. That is not to say that all the references are good! Ben will just as easily talk about my stubbornness as my shyness. So anyway, Ben had just finished preaching, and Professor Bob asked him who I was because Ben kept talking about me in his sermon. I was making my way to Ben when Professor Bob asked, "Is this Gloria?"

"Yes, this is Gloria, my wife," Ben answered.

Bob took out his camera. "Let me take your photograph."

He took our photograph. Then he said, "Please, say yes that you will come to America and do a doctorate in theology. You will be very well taken care of. Just say yes!"

Ben and I looked at him and at each other, stunned.

Bob continued. "Look, I know the head of the Anglican department in the Luther Northwestern Seminary. They have more money than the Lutherans, and I will make sure some of that money goes to you and Gloria, if you say yes to doing a doctorate."

Just like that. We smiled at Bob and made all the right noises. Inwardly, we were both thinking the same thing. *Of course, universities handed out doctoral scholarships just like that! Of course it was that easy! These Americans, bless their generous but completely impractical hearts!*

A year later in 1990, we received a letter from Luther Northwestern Theological Seminary. The letter said that Ben and I had been admitted to the university on a full scholarship worth US$66,000. They had also made allowances for our children. By this time, I was pregnant with my third child, and our family would soon include two adopted children, Pangak and Nendelmwa.

We were stunned. So the professor had been serious! Yes, we had been in sporadic contact with him over the past year, but Ben and I never thought for a minute that his offer would come to anything. It sounds terrible, but it's the truth. We just thought we were humouring the professor because he was so keen and convinced that this was the right thing for us.

We hadn't even applied for the course. But the scholarship was ours. All we needed to do was fill in the application forms (talk about doing things backwards), get them endorsed by our bishop, and we were US-bound. Easy as that – except the bishop part.

Ben took the forms to our bishop, Titus Ogbonyomi, who was like a father to us.

"Ben," Bishop Ogbonyomi told my husband gently. "It's not the right time. Defer it."

"Baba, I can't," Ben said. "I'll lose the scholarship."

In African culture, Baba is a term of deference to a wise, older man.

"Well," Baba said. "If you don't want to write to them, then I will on your behalf."

True to his word, Baba wrote to the seminary, and against all expectations and scholarship procedure, they agreed to defer the scholarship by another year.

In 1991, Ben was asked to go to the Middle East as part of a team to investigate whether Kaduna, one of the states in northern Nigeria, could send Christian pilgrims there. Such is the nature of religious sensitivity in Nigeria that the government allocates a certain percentage of its budget for Christian and Muslim pilgrimages.

When the team flew back to Nigeria, I went to meet Ben at the airport.

"The bishop wants to see you," I said.

We went straight to Kaduna to see the bishop. When we arrived, I left Bishop Ogbonyomi and Ben together so that they could talk in private. The bishop handed him a letter. It was handwritten in ink. It said the church of God had met under the leadership of the Holy Spirit and Ben had been elected to the See of Jos. The decision was passed by a vote of the House of Bishops and signed by the primate of the Anglican Church of Nigeria, who at that time was Archbishop Joseph Abiodun Adetiloye.

"But sir," Ben told our bishop. "I am going to the US to study for my doctorate."

The bishop didn't say much. All he said was, "Well ..."

On the one hand, this was great news. But on the other, there was the doctorate. My husband was confused. We wondered, *Lord, what to do?*

Bishop Ogbonyomi was a very wise man. He said, "You know, the church has prayed, so this appointment must come from God. And you know the church in Jos has had a lot of problems. God has equipped and prepared you for this."

He spoke gently to my husband. Then he prayed with him.

Ben said, "Sir, I don't like keeping anything from my wife."

"Yes, you can tell Gloria about the appointment. I know she's discreet. But make sure you both keep it to yourselves. In the meantime, pray together. And if you still think you don't want the bishopric, then reply straight away to the primate. But I'm telling you now, you can do this."

That gave us a week of breathing space. We found out later that all the others who had been elected bishops had accepted their elections, but the primate couldn't make the announcement because Ben was away and had not written an acceptance. Nor were they sure he would accept.

I prayed with my husband about what we should do. But in my heart of hearts I knew what I wanted to do: I wanted to go to the US and start afresh. By this time, I was pregnant with our fourth child, and everything about the scholarship ticked the right boxes. One of Ben's sisters, Caroline, lived an hour away from the seminary. She is a doctor, and the hospital she worked for wasn't too far from the seminary either. Her father-in-law had sold us his car for a dollar (yes, US$1). Everything was all set up. Ben's other sister, Anna, actually lived in the same city as the campus. So we were not without family in the USA.

The Venerable D. Odigie, Archbishop Ben and Gloria at the end of the Women's Guild and Mothers' Union conference, 2012

Moreover, I was tired of church politics. The Jos church wasn't dead, but it wasn't an attractive church. They were known for their in-fighting and for suing each other. The church also had a lot of tribal politics. Even worse, they had the highest number of secret occult societies in the Anglican Church of Nigeria. So everything was just ...

I was tired of the grafting. I was tired! Tired! *Tired!* In some way I believed that God was calling us to study.

We prayed for the answer. One of the people on Ben's prayer team was Dr Bitrus Gani, a blind physician. He and Ben had been prayer partners for years. His prayer team had also been praying for days. One day as they were praying, Dr Gani said, "Ben, this is what the Lord said: 'America is the window, Jos is the door'. And Jesus said, 'I am the door'."

So that was that.

8

THE BISHOP OF JOS

Ben came home from the prayer meeting and told me what Dr Gani had told him. I accepted it immediately. Well, in my head I accepted it. It took a while for my emotions to accept it – *so much for a fresh start*, I thought. But long ago, I made up my mind to serve the Lord no matter what. If he, the Alpha and Omega, had decreed that Jos was the door, then who was I to argue with him?

Ben wrote his letter of acceptance to the primate. He was consecrated as the Bishop of Jos on 9 February 1992. The day after the consecration, we started work.

A month before the consecration, we had our fourth child and named him Arbet, a name that in Ben's language means "The door for the gospel has opened" – because of the word from the Lord for Ben's bishopric.

I'll let Ben tell you about the Diocese of Jos.

The Diocese of Jos

I, Ben, am from Jos in the Plateau State. My birthplace is about a ninety minute drive from where I now live. I know this place, and I know the people who live here. My heart beats for these people. But, for you to understand the problems I faced, you need to know something of the history of the church in Jos.

In 1907, Anglican missionaries from the Church Missionary Society (CMS) evangelized the Plateau. They did such great work that they not only covered most of the Plateau State but also went into the surrounding states like Bauchi and some areas where the Ibo people lived in Taraba State.

But, in about 1930, the CMS missionaries had to leave because of an agreement their mission had made with the Sudan United Mission (SUM) and the Sudan Interior Mission (SIM). These mission organizations (and a few others) had agreed to divide up the work in the north of Nigeria, giving each one a specific geographical area to work in. The SUM wanted to work in Jos, and so the CMS handed over the area to them. This type of arrangement was strongly encouraged by the colonial government, who didn't want missions competing with each other. They encouraged each mission to have its own territory. However, these arrangements were disliked by many of the local people, and broke down under the weight of urbanization, for migrants who moved to cities wanted to worship in the types of churches they were familiar with.

The SUM operated very differently from the CMS. The CMS educated the local people and was keen to provide them with healthcare and training. The SUM, by contrast, was eager to please the British governor of Nigeria, Lord Lugard. It listened when he told their missionaries to go only to rural places and not to upset the Muslims in the north. This was because Lord Lugard had entered into an agreement with the emirs, promising that missions would not work in Muslim areas but would concentrate their work in areas where the traditional religion was dominant. That is why there were so few mission stations in the Islamic cities in northern Nigeria. Yet in the past CMS missionaries had been welcomed in Muslim areas. The Emir of Zaria had welcomed them into the city and given them a large expanse of land in Wusasa on the outskirts of Zaria. There were many theories about why he did this. Some people say it was to keep them out of the heart of the city, where their first mission station had been located. But others believe they were given the huge expanse of land in recognition of the good work they were doing.

Although the CMS had officially left northern Nigeria, Anglican congregations persisted, and even grew as a result of the work of native evangelists. For example, St Paul's Anglican Church in Pankshin became a fully established congregation in 1936, but received no pastoral care and oversight. Many people don't realize that there were already Anglican churches in Jos in 1930. They were led by Ibo and Yoruba priests who came to Jos to minister to the people of their tribes. It would have taken them only one hour's drive or less to look after the other indigenous congregations that the CMS Anglicans had started, but these priests chose to ignore them.

The Yoruba and Ibo Anglicans neglect of their fellow Anglicans meant that quite a number of indigenous churches in the area were without pastoral care for a very long time. As a result, many of them went back to traditional, animist practices. They were all but forgotten by the wider world until Tiyus Ogbonyomi became Bishop of Northern Nigeria in 1976. He was an evangelist at heart and a Northerner. As he travelled around his vast diocese he discovered an indigenous Anglican church that had refused to accept the leadership of the SUM in 1930. From 1930 until 1975, when Bishop Ogbonyomi discovered them, they had been without spiritual leadership and pastoral ministry.

Can you imagine, an indigenous church without pastoral care for almost fifty years! What do you think happened? There were polygamous marriages. They imbibed alcohol freely. They did all these things and still professed adherence to the Anglican Church.

Bishop Ogbonyomi realized that the problem was too large for him to tackle on his own, and asked to have the Diocese of Northern Nigeria broken up into three smaller dioceses: Kaduna, Jos and Kano.

That was in 1980. The newly created Diocese of Jos covered Benue, Plateau, Taraba and Adamawa states. Most of the churches were located in the academic and business areas of major cities and served primarily Ibo and Yoruba congregations. But the diocese also included a number of the neglected indigenous churches on the Plateau.

The first Bishop of Jos, Samuel Ebo, was from the Ibo tribe. He had been led to believe that the Ibo were the majority tribe in the Anglican Church in Jos, which riled the Yoruba who made up most of the congregation in the cathedral there and sparked a crisis between the Yoruba and the Ibo in the Jos diocese.

Five years later, Bishop Samuel Ebo was moved to another diocese, and a Yoruba man, Timothy Adesola, became the Bishop of Jos. He had been ordained in Jos in 1955, so he knew northern Nigeria very well. But he was also a Yoruba and not an indigene from Jos. The Ibos were not happy. The diocese was torn apart and the Ibo and Yoruba ended up suing each other for control and ownership of the cathedral and other assets.

It was a right mess.

In the meantime, the local indigenous people, who were neither Ibo nor Yoruba, and who had endured general neglect since colonial days, were asking, "What's all this fight over the cathedral about?" So they also entered the fray and the in-fighting got worse. Subdividing the diocese still further did nothing to help the situation.

This was the mess I inherited when I was appointed Bishop of Jos in 1992.

I suspect that one of the reasons for my appointment was that I came from Jos. Many people assume that I am from the Yoruba tribe of southwest Nigeria. Others assume that I belong to the predominantly Muslim Hausa tribe in northern Nigeria. But actually I am an indigene from Jos. The bishops hoped that as such I would be able to clear up the mess.

I was known for being an evangelist, more specifically, a bush evangelist. So some of the older bishops had misgivings about my ability to the work and handle all the politics of being a bishop. But that was what the archbishop was looking for: an evangelist who would concentrate on serving the church alone.

Being the Bishop of Jos

When I was consecrated, I knew exactly what I was getting into, and we knew what our focus would be: local, indigenous missions and a Christ-centred Anglican Church in Jos. So on 10 February, the day after my consecration, I called a meeting of the clergy (about seventeen of them, I believe) in the cathedral and told them the three key areas I believed God was asking me to work in: 1) evangelism; 2) community building (schools, hospitals, community development, and building relations between Christians and Muslims); and 3) community leadership.

I was handed the constitution of Jos diocese, which included the titles of the officers of the cathedral: vicar-general, provost of the cathedral, canon chapters – both upper and lower ... It was madness. I thought, *No wonder they are at each other's throats!*

"Is this how you run a cathedral?" I asked.

I was told that because I had never run a cathedral, I wouldn't have knowledge of such matters. Besides, the cathedral was governed by canons and constitutions that I had to follow. Not to worry, they said, they would tell me what to do. The clergy went on like this for a while and I listened.

"By the way, there's also an appointments committee," they said, "and other committees – and we need to talk about those."

"Really?" I asked.

"Yes," they said.

"Okay, well, put this on record," I said. "I, the Bishop of Jos by divine permission, declare this constitution suspended. Thank you very much."

The meeting didn't last twenty minutes. I told them to note it down as an official record that I was now the pastor of the cathedral, and that I didn't need the organizational paraphernalia attached to the cathedral.

Then, I said, "Okay. I thank you very much."

The clergy sat there looking at me. So I thought I would make things clearer.

"You know what? The board is dissolved as well. Right, shall we pray? Any comments?"

We prayed, the board was dissolved, and I dismissed the meeting.

The next day, I also dissolved all the archdeaconries and deaneries within the diocese and asked that all the bank books be brought to me. Jos was one diocese and one archdeaconry with one bishop.

I told the clergy, "If you don't want to work with me, that's fine. But for now, there is no constitution, no archdeacon, no nothing. I don't want or need anyone."

At the meeting, the Yorubas and the Ibos had spoken in their own languages, not realizing that I could speak Yoruba and also understood Ibo. They said they would stand back and watch my suicide mission. Very soon, this silly young boy would come to his senses, they thought.

I enjoyed the challenge.

I took drastic action because it was necessary. The church was in a parlous state, and sometimes you have to knock down to rebuild. That was exactly what I was doing.

Over the next two years, I travelled all over my diocese. I established friendships with the Muslim emirs, kings, chiefs and district heads. I visited every district and district head. I prayed for people and shared with them what I believed God had laid on my heart for Jos. I also tried to establish relationships with other denominations.

Soon we had gone six years without a constitution, a committee and an archdeaconry. In those years, the diocese had also grown from 85 to 195 Anglican churches. These were churches with thriving indigenous and Christ-centred congregations and clergy. The number of clergy had also increased from seventeen to eighty-eight.

We did great with evangelism, too. Dynamic young preachers and their determined wives went into the bush villages to evangelize, and they did a great job. They organized rallies, made strong links in the communities and established churches.

Our financial situation also improved. We used to struggle to pay salaries, but now we could pay clergy and staff. In those six years we also established about six secondary schools and about four primary schools and started the Christian Institute, a seminary for training teachers, health workers, Christians who want to work in the media, and pastors.

Those were busy and challenging times. But God was with us. We had people supporting us who donated money for various projects. I remember the very first time this happened. We needed a mode of transport that would help our "foot soldiers", the evangelists, go into the bush to fulfil their calling. An army general heard about our need and gave us about half a million naira (US$3,000) to buy bicycles and motorcycles. I wish you could have seen how the foot soldiers put them to use. It was – and still is – a beautiful sight to behold.

Gloria is not one to sit back and be idle. She was very much involved in the "Great March". She would gather a group of women and disappear for days and weeks in remote communities, preaching and establishing churches and schools.

As the drive for evangelism and community building gained momentum, people talked less and less of court cases. Of their own volition, they started to forgive each other and withdraw the court cases. The work grew so much that we even had to split off part of it to create a new diocese, Lafia Diocese, in Nasarawa State that borders Jos.

After six years, I called another meeting of the clergy.

"Now, we can set up a committee to look into setting up a really simple constitution," I said. "I don't want anything confusing. I'm not interested in upper or lower chapters. Those things belong to England. In any case, that organization hasn't worked for them, so it certainly won't work for us here in Nigeria! I am not a church killer, so if something is killing the English church, I don't want it. I only want the things that will grow the church."

I have often wondered why ex-colonies hold on to rituals and traditions from other places that have no part in their native culture. It galls me no end: *Why do we import things that will not work?!*

By 1999 we had a much simpler constitution, one that anybody could read and understand, and most importantly, we used the Nigerian culture as our frame of reference. There are bits of it that I think aren't that clear, but that's lawyers for you!

In the next eight years, we established over 300 congregations.

Not that "we" did this. The Lord knows my and Gloria's heart. He has seen us on our knees when we have cried to him for Jos and northern Nigeria. We pray daily against the increasing intolerance to Christianity in the region, and we ask the Lord's forgiveness for the incessant nitpicking of church politics that draws our attention away from what is important: serving people.

Front: Nendelmwa, Gloria, Ben, Nanminen and Pangak
Rear: Hannatu, Arbet and Rinji

9

RAISING THE BISHOP'S CHILDREN

I have always had a thirst for knowledge. I just like finding out things. A running joke in my family is that wherever a course is being taught, there I will be. This is the reason they call me a "coursite".

I think the reason I like to take courses is because I believe that we should always maintain a healthy curiosity and gain knowledge about life for ourselves and to share with others. Without knowledge, how will we grow as individuals and communities? The Bible says that "my people are destroyed from lack of knowledge" (Hosea 4:6). Well, I've seen this for myself in my work and in the lives of people around me.

I saw it in my home village of Numan, where young girls died in backstreet abortion clinics at the hands of butchers.

I saw it in seminary, where people did not respect the knowledge they were being given and subsequently made bad decisions.

I saw it in the villages and cities where we were posted. People were fed the wrong information and indoctrinated with the wrong type of knowledge, which led to the killing of innocent people.

But I have also seen the power of knowledge – what it can do and how it can bring change. This kind of knowledge is preached in Christ-centred churches all over the world. It empowers, never imprisons, and always seeks to bring spiritual and consequently external transformation in the lives of individuals and those around them. That is the power of the gospel. That is the power that I long for and seek when I take these courses in my quest as a "coursite".

My husband and children know when I have been touched by a course because I come back with my brain on fire, a stupid grin on my face and my eyes all lit up like firecrackers. When this happens, they roll their eyes and think, "Here we go again. What is she going to do now?"

But I don't just love learning. I also love being a wife and mother. When I think of where I have come from, I am so thankful to God for doing far above anything I could ever ask or even think of receiving from him. After all, I had never ever expected to be married at all, let alone to be married for thirty years to a man like Ben, a man with a heart that burns with passion for God and people – and has the ability to make me laugh!

When Ben and I had children, we were deeply concerned about the so-called curse of pastors' children. Okay, fine. There isn't a curse per se. More a so-called inevitability about pastors' children abandoning the faith they grew up with. I was determined that my children would not fall into that category. I was going to raise godly children who would serve God and be of use to him and the people around them.

Schooling the Children

I was also inspired by a Scottish missionary, Shina Harris, who was a member of our church in Zaria. One day, she told me she was studying. I asked Ben why she was studying at her age, and he said it was because she wanted to homeschool her children through high school. I had to find out how to do that, and so I asked her about it. She then said something so profound that it completely changed the way I looked at parenting. She said, "You train a child only once in life, but you can get a job or go to school any time in your life." That statement stuck in my mind.

I had always admired missionary children. The ones I knew seemed so well-behaved and knowledgeable. They didn't attend the local schools but were homeschooled by their parents. I really wanted to homeschool my children, but when I tried I did it so badly that I had to stop. The primary reason I failed was that I lacked the knowledge to do it effectively.

So instead of homeschooling them, Ben and I put our children in the best school we could afford. But we had no end of problems. For example, Rinji, my second child and first son, seemed to have an innate ability to incite hatred from his teachers. He must have been about five years old in 1992 when his father was made bishop, and Rinji was bullied and beaten up pretty badly by one of the teachers in his primary school because he was the bishop's child. Hannatu, my first child and daughter, wasn't doing too well either because she was bullied on account of her weight.

In that same year, I was introduced to something called Accelerated Christian Education (ACE). I went to their two-week course, and at the end of it I told a friend that we should get our children together and start homeschooling them. I enthusiastically told Ben about my plans.

"Hmm, I don't like this," he said. "Every time you go to a training course, you come back all bright-eyed and full of ideas."

But that isn't my fault. I just like learning new things.

Eventually Ben agreed, and I started the homeschooling. A month later, the children started reading. It wasn't long before we added more children – our children's friends and others from the neighbouring community – to our home school. All in all, we had about fifteen children.

I homeschooled my children for about six years, until they went to secondary school at age eleven. However, I haven't stopped. I still homeschool children today. Some are from poorer neighbouring communities, and others are my adopted children. We average about 270 children on a school day, so I don't do it on my own any more. We have about five helpers, including my sister-in-law who is a trained teacher. Their salary isn't good, but they persevere because they can see that what we are doing is good. To pay them we use the proceeds of a communion wafer business that I initially set up as a way for widows to earn money. But the business has grown to support our ministry with children.

Not all the children are from Christian homes. Some are Muslims. I don't shy away from declaring my faith and the reason I chose to homeschool my children, but I don't consciously seek to convert the other children from the surrounding communities. I reason that they already know my religious beliefs.

Gloria for a Mother – Hannatu's Perspective

Growing up, I never quite understood my mum because she wasn't affectionate. I wanted a mother who would hug and kiss me, but my mum is not that way inclined. I think that is why I believe that her marriage with my dad is truly a God-thing, because my dad is the exact opposite. He's affectionate and romantic. Sometimes when he does things for my mum and she starts going off about his spending money, blah, blah, blah, I get annoyed. "Mum!" I say. "How many Nigerian husbands would do what Dad has just done? Just shut up, accept the romantic gesture and enjoy it!"

For a long time, I felt my mother was a hard woman. She was always in my face saying, "You must do this. You must do that." She would go through my things, and we were always at loggerheads. I just wanted her to leave me alone, because it seemed to me that I couldn't please her.

We had to bathe every morning, and my mother would rub Mentholatum all over us to soften our skins and protect us from the cold, because Jos is about 4,000 feet above sea-level and it can be cold. We didn't see her rubbing Mentholatum all over us as love, because we didn't like it. But then we were children, so what did we know?

There were a lot of soap operas on television in Nigeria. A really popular one was called, "The Rich Also Cry". Well, I never got to see it because it wasn't "Christian". What I did see a lot of was "The Sound of Music" and "Veggie Tales": good, wholesome entertainment. But when you are a kid, you don't want to watch those movies. You want to watch what your friends are watching so you can swap stories with each other in school.

Mum also took us out of primary school and homeschooled all of us until we were ready to go to secondary school. That was no mean feat. Our family had grown to more than six because my cousins had also joined our family. We were effectively raised as brothers and sisters – which is how we see each other. Waking us all, bathing us, feeding us breakfast, then homeschool, lunch ... Imagine teaching your child something ten times over. My mother also taught other children in the neighbourhood. That couldn't have been easy. I sometimes lead Sunday school, and I know how tedious it can be to repeat things and try to make the lessons interactive and interesting.

When I was at secondary school, my friends would talk about watching a movie with their mums or going on shopping trips. I would just sit there, silent, because I didn't have any such stories. My mother is not that way inclined. I'm sure if I had suggested it, she would have done those things with me. But that's not who my mum is. She likes to be busy doing stuff, being useful. Her idea of hell would be just sitting down to watch a movie. She would be bored within minutes. Not to say that she doesn't go on shopping trips or watch films at all. It's just that she would rather be doing other things.

When I was at secondary school as a boarder, mum would go through my things. I was only allowed to take what the school allowed, nothing more. But other parents colluded with their children to smuggle in what they felt their daughters needed or wanted. I didn't lack anything at school, but I never had the luxury of being rebellious. If I needed anything, I would write home. But it would have been nice to be able to break the rules, or at least try to break them!

Then I went off to study medicine in the Ukraine. There I heard many of my friends blaming their parents for many things. Chief amongst their complaints was the lack of time their parents spent with them. Even when they went home to Nigeria, their parents didn't have time for them.

I didn't have such complaints. My mother made sure that we bathed twice a day. She was always there, right from the minute I was born to the time I went to secondary school as a boarder. I thought she was in my face. But in Ukraine, the veil was pulled from my eyes and I saw, I mean I really saw, my mother for who she is. I remember thinking, *Wow, so that's what it means to love and take care of your child!*

In Ukraine, I would sometimes sit with my Nigerian friends and sing Christian songs or retell Bible stories that they didn't have a clue about. But it wasn't only my student friends who didn't know the Bible. Even some elders in the church Bible study I attended didn't know these stories. When I recounted them, they would say, "Wow, how did you know this?"

And I would reply: "I learnt it at Sunday school."

If you don't learn these basics when you are young, it is quite difficult to pick them up as an adult Christian. So I began to appreciate all that my mum had taught me all those years ago.

Now, when I look through my baby pictures, I never once see a picture in which I was dirty or anything like that. And when I see the kind of filth children watch now on television or the videos their parents allow them to rent, I remember my mother's quality control of what I watched, and I really, really thank God that she protected my young mind. I wonder how it will be possible for me to give my own children the love and care my mother showered on me.

Now my mum and I are very close. She is honest, and she tells me everything. She shares her heart with me: her problems and her pains. We pray together. I can tell her my heart, and if I'm angry about anything, I can tell her and she actually takes it. I'm so humbled to see how we've grown together.

Now she is my hero!

A Bishop for a Father – Hannatu's Perspective

Dad is my father, but he is also my friend and my pastor. In many ways, he modelled God to me. For example, I have never forgotten the lesson I learnt from an incident that happened when I was in my second-last year at boarding school.

It was what we called "visiting day", a day when parents could come and see their children, usually once a month. A friend's mother told me that she had met my dad, and he had told her that he was coming to see me that day. My dad travels quite frequently, so when the woman told me that he would come that visiting day, I knew he was in town.

"Why don't you eat something?" my friend's mother asked.

"No, thank you. I'll wait for my dad," I replied.

You see, when my mum came to visit, she brought home-cooked, wholesome food, which is fine. But I loved it even more when my dad came, because he would bring junk food: chocolates, crisps and all the other rubbish that I love.

So when my friend's mother offered some of her home-made food, I had to decline because I was saving myself for the junk food my wonderful father would surely bring.

This was in the morning.

Lunchtime came and went, and still no dad.

One of our family friends had a child in the school as well. "Are you sure your father is coming?" she asked.

"Yes," I answered.

"Eat."

"No, thank you. I'm waiting for my father."

By this time, I was ravenous. But I wasn't going to eat anything until I had seen my dad.

Visiting day officially ended at 6 p.m. After that, the school gates closed. 4:00 p.m., 5:00 p.m., 6:00 p.m. The school gates closed. I went indoors, depressed.

About 6:30 p.m., I couldn't take it anymore. I burst out crying. People crowded around me thinking I was upset because nobody had come to see me. I went to see our house mistress and told her I wanted to go home.

"There's a problem. My father has died," I said. And I really did believe it. "If he is not dead, then he has been in an accident or something. But something has definitely happened!"

"Don't say that. It's not true. Maybe your father forgot …"

"He didn't forget" I snapped. "He keeps his word. He didn't forget. He even told somebody that he was coming to see me."

"Well, you know your father is very busy …"

But I wasn't interested in what she had to say.

"I want to go home. NOW!"

She thought I was joking.

So I cried even harder. They got really worried. I was summoned to the headmaster's house.

"We'll call your house with the landline. At least you will be able to talk to your father and know everything's okay," he said.

They called my home landline. The call didn't go through.

I started bawling.

"Something's happened. My father is a man of his word. I must go home, TONIGHT!!"

The headmaster got really angry and started shouting. "You are not going anywhere."

When he realized that his shouting made things worse, he and my house mistress started making arrangements for one of the on-site teachers to take me home. Deep inside, he was thinking, *Perhaps she is right. Maybe something has happened to the bishop.*

About 8:00 p.m., while they were still making arrangements to take me home, a car drove up the headmaster's driveway. He went out to see who it was, and there stood my dad with my mum, talking to the house mistress. The headmaster just stood with his mouth open. I looked through the school window, saw my dad and went outside.

"I told you he would come!" I said. "The only reason he wouldn't have come was if something was wrong."

The headmaster stood there dumbfounded. Dad explained that they had gone to the burial of one of our family friends. As they were coming back, they had a flat tire. By then it was evening. Mum had said to him, "You know what? Let's just go home, and we'll come back. She will understand."

But my dad refused, "No," he replied. "I've already promised her that we're coming, so we are going to make it."

Now, I can remind myself, "If my earthly father can keep his promises, and if my earthly father can forgive me and tell me the truth, then how much more God ..."

Dad also taught us what it means to discipline someone in love. I know that many Westerners disapprove of spanking children, but that idea is not shared in Africa. However, before spanking us, he would talk to us. "Why did you do that?" he would ask. "Do you understand the consequences of what you have done? How are you going to make amends?"

When we fully understood why he was going to spank us, dad would send us to a room and tell us exactly what he was going to do: "I'm going to give you six strokes, and there is nothing you can do about it. It is going to happen. But I need you to understand why I've decided on six strokes, not three."

He taught me to trust that he was fair and that God, too, could discipline us in love. Now I can see God as a father, and as a friend.

Dad was also someone I could talk to about everything – from the Nigerian Civil War to marijuana. In fact, my main complaint about him is that it is difficult for me to date a man without comparing him to my father! He has set a high standard for a loving relationship.

Not that we were indulged. Some of my worst times were when I was studying in the Ukraine because I really struggled financially. My dad was so strict with me. He would send me US$500 and that was meant to last for six months. My last year before graduation was awful. Most of the time the money was not enough, so I just wanted to come home. At least in Nigeria if I was broke, I would still be able to eat.

My father would say, "Honey, if I send you $2,000 a month, you'll find that when you start working, you won't earn that much. This amount of money makes sense, you know."

It also made sense because he himself was living on a clergyman's salary. But sometimes I would get a joyous message, "I preached at such and such place, and God was so good. The church blessed me with some money, so I'll be able to pay for your ticket to come home." He shared his blessings with me, but I also had to learn to be prudent.

10

WALKING WITH GLORIA

In the early years of our marriage, every time we moved, once I had finished setting up our new home, I would just go walking. I can't sit still. And the miracle of it is that when I do go out, I always find someone, somewhere who needs my help.

This has sometimes led me into major areas of ministry. For example, I can remember how our school ministry began in Zaria in 1984.

Within the first week of moving into my new home there, I decided that I needed to find out more about the area. So I started walking. I walked for three hours, just strolling and taking note of my surroundings. I saw a village on the horizon and decided to walk towards it. Eventually, I got tired because I didn't seem to be getting any closer. However, en route I met some people with whom I started speaking. I also saw many children wandering about doing nothing. Just wandering ...

"Shouldn't you be in school?" I asked them.

Their answers were all the same, "My parents cannot afford it."

"If I came back and decided to teach you how to read, would you like that?"

They all nodded. So I came back. It wasn't long before I would have a crowd of about 250 people sitting in on my classes. People find that figure very hard to believe, but in northern Nigeria, it was – and still is – very easy to gather a crowd. I would start teaching a group of children under some trees, and soon one or two people would come and watch. Then more and more people would join in. It wasn't long before the crowd would swell to 250. Unemployment levels were high in the villages, so people had nothing to do. My classes were a break from the day-to-day tedium.

I remember telling people to go away because the children couldn't concentrate with such a crowd surrounding them. If I tried teaching the kids, a rumble would go through the crowd in waves.

"What is she saying to the kids? Who is she?" the people would ask, and then they would come closer, much to my frustration. When I didn't know what else to do, I invited them to join us, and some did.

I taught in that village for a few hours every other day – whenever I could get some time off from the seminary. Soon, whenever the children saw me approach the village, they would shout, "Aunty is here!"

I would also tell them stories about Jesus Christ. I didn't want their parents to think I was evangelizing their children. But in my heart, I believe that everyone should have an opportunity to hear about Jesus, and who knew if I was the one God had appointed as his messenger to these children? So I would tell them about Jesus and other Bible stories in ways they could understand.

Zambiri School. After constructing the feeding centre and classrooms, we got uniforms for the children. A quarter of these children live in our home while the rest live with other relations or guardians we have made responsible for them.

Ben and I know first-hand the power of education and how it can transform lives, and so this experience in the village set a pattern for us. To date, Ben and I have established about twenty primary schools and sixteen secondary schools in Jos diocese. Elsewhere in northern

Nigeria, we have established five primary schools, one health school, one secondary and a tertiary school – the Christian Institute.

This ministry matches the commission the Lord has given to Ben: "Christ first, then education, and last community building (schools, farming, and improving Christian-Muslim relations)." So in reality, we are just obeying the Lord and doing as he has instructed us to do. It is surely his grace – and I must admit, Ben's and my stubbornness – that has enabled us to get this far. As you have read in these pages, the journey has not been a smooth or easy one. But we are not complaining. I know that if we had the chance to do it all over again, we would.

It wasn't only on my walks that I met people who needed help. I remember once Ben and I were driving in our car. The clouds gathered and the heavens opened. It was the kind of torrential rain that has been known to sweep away whole communities. As we drove, we passed a woman who was carrying a baby. I looked again – the baby couldn't have been more than a week old. She was strapped on her mother's back with a cloth wrap. On the mother's head was a load of firewood.

My heart sank.

"That could have been me," I said. I was remembering the story of my birth. How I had been born on the roadside on a market day when it had rained terribly hard, and my mother had used rain water to wash me before wrapping me in rags and putting me in a basin that she carried on her head.

I was not at peace, but we drove on for another two kilometres (one and a half miles) while I went on and on at Ben.

"What if that woman had been me? What if?"

"Gloria, here we go again. We can't just pick up women from the street!"

I still went on at him. "What if it was me out there, being battered by the rain, with our child strapped to my back? What if, what if?"

Finally, Ben relented, and we went back to pick up the woman and her baby. I was so happy! The woman was so grateful. We went past other people, men with their horses and all that, but I didn't much care about them. My concern had been for that baby, who as it turned out was just a few days old. We took the woman and the baby to our home where they rested and left when the rain eased off.

People often ask me why I do things like that. I say it's because God has put these people in my heart, and usually I'm not at peace until I obey. This behaviour has got me into trouble, though!

I have been on my famous walks and come back with an ex-convict whose stories of repentance were really just that, stories.

Another time, Ben and I had been out walking near the church when I saw a woman carrying a baby on her back and holding another. She said she had been stranded, and it was too late for her to go back home. Well, we lived in the church, and our policy is to never turn anyone away. So we brought her in and I bathed her and her children and gave them some food. Eventually, they went to sleep in the spare room. When we woke up at 6:00 a.m. to pray, I went to knock on the bedroom door for her to join us. To cut a long story short, we found out that she had robbed us. She totally cleared out our home. To this day, I don't know how she managed to rob our house and leave in the early hours of the morning with two young children, and the children didn't make a sound. It was and still is a mystery.

But did I learn from that experience? No! As long as there are people in need, I will reach out, just as God reached out to me all those years ago when I was born and when I became a Christian in secondary school.

I have also been known to see children fighting in the streets, stop my car, step out and tell them off. When they stop, I don't drive away but will sometimes follow them to make sure they don't continue the fight elsewhere. I won't have any peace in my heart until I do this. I have been told that all these things mean that God has definitely given me a ministry to women and little children.

My name is Gloria, and as long as I live, my desire is to have God's glory and grace reflected in my life. I hope and pray that my work with women and children reflects that glory.

I do minister to men as well. Once I drove past some builders close to my house. I was in a bit of a hurry, as I had an appointment to get to. But as I passed, I saw the builders taking sheets of zinc roofing material from the building site and loading them into an *okada*, a motorcycle taxi. Then they went back into the house to do the work they were contracted to do.

I have been known to complain to God, "I just want to do good things and not see the bad. So why do you insist on showing me bad things? And you know that I won't keep quiet. I'll get something done." Whether it's helping a victim or confronting criminals – I will do something about the situation. So when I saw what the builders were doing, it did not sit right with me at all.

I don't quite know when I decided to follow the okada. When the driver turned to look at me, his look just confirmed my suspicions. It also strengthened my resolve to follow him.

It wasn't like I didn't have things to do. I did. But I was so uneasy about what I had seen that following that okada driver to see what he would do with the stack of zinc he had been given became my most important task of the day. I prayed, "God, I have no idea how this is going to end. But you have shown it to me, and how it concludes is entirely up to you."

The okada driver started speeding, and I did the same. At one point, he looked around, trying to find a way to cut me off. So I sped up my car, cornered him on the road so he had no room to manoeuvre, wound down my window and said, "Where are you taking those bundles of zinc?"

At first he didn't want to answer me. I asked him again, louder this time, and he answered reluctantly, "They told me to take it to XXX."

I pretended that I owned the zinc and commanded the driver to return to the building site with me following him. When I arrived there, I had harsh words for the foreman.

"You ought to be ashamed of yourself. You've got all your apprentices with you, and here you are, stealing zinc and other building materials from the guy you are building for. So from the start, your apprentices are doomed, because they'll learn horrible, evil practices from you. The poor man whose house you are building, who has probably carefully budgeted the amount of money he needs for his precious house, will be short-changed because you have stolen his zinc. And now you will do shoddy work on his house with the scant remains of his materials. Have you no fear of God?"

The men were terrified and started begging me for forgiveness. I gave them another lecture and went on to my appointment. I arrived late, but it didn't matter. The Lord had shown me a situation, and I had responded. I was happy.

But I digress.

11

THE ORPHANAGE

As I have said, I like to take courses. In 1999 I went to a workshop on community development in Bauchi, about 127 kilometres (80 miles) from Jos. During the introductions, I told everyone my name and the organization I was representing, the Mothers' Union. This is an international charity of the Anglican Church that aims to empower women by teaching them what it means to lead the Christian life and giving them the skills to do it. In many Anglican churches, the pastor's wife is, by default, the leader of the Mothers' Union.

Among those attending the workshop was a white woman, who introduced herself as representing another group that worked with women and children in Jos and Kaduna.

"What's the Mothers' Union?" she asked me.

I told her that it was a Christian organization that worked with women and children.

"My group is for social workers," she said. "We don't do religion."

As we talked, I became aware that she seemed to have the organizational skills that I lacked when it came to running the Mothers' Union. So I invited her to drop by for a visit. It wasn't long before we started calling and writing to each other. We became friends. She would invite me to attend workshops that she organized for children's workers. They called it child-to-child training. From where I stood, it looked very like an Accelerated Christian Education (ACE) programme. I had homeschooled all my children using that model, so I do know what I'm talking about. Child-to-child training is children learning and teaching themselves and sharing with each other.

My new friend was an American and so she often travelled to the USA to raise funds for her organization. It was a huge operation requiring much work. She ran four orphanages in cities in two states in Nigeria, offering shelter to vulnerable children of all ages, including children who were HIV-positive or had been labelled autistic. She helped women. She arranged for HIV tests and then helped those who tested positive to access anti-retroviral drugs. She was doing the work that native Nigerians should have been doing.

You can imagine how tiring her work was. So whenever Jane came to visit, I would encourage her to spend a few days at my house just to rest. We also did some work together, going into villages, conducting HIV tests and encouraging villagers to keep their HIV-free status.

What's Wrong?

I remember the first time I visited one of her orphanages. I'm sorry to say this, but it didn't make a good impression. I've always felt that if children are living in a home – even if they are poor – they should be able to take pride in their home. But the area around the orphanage was filled with dead leaves and rubbish. I live with children, and I know they can drive you crazy. But if the younger ones couldn't do the gardening, then surely the older ones could have done it? I knew something was wrong, but I didn't know what.

I averted my eyes from the untidy surroundings and consoled myself with the thought that the fallen leaves would eventually turn into compost.

Then I went inside the orphanage. It was partitioned into flats. My friend and her husband lived in one of the flats, and the children and their helpers lived in the others. A woman, one of the helpers, was carrying a baby on her back. There were also some grown children, about fifteen of them I think.

After that, I visited the orphanage occasionally. But from 2004 on, my visits became more frequent. There was trouble in the city, ethnic and religious tensions were rising, a curfew was in place, and my friend was in America on one of her fundraising expeditions. She had been gone a long time, and I had begun to hear stories about the orphanage that disturbed me.

I started visiting the children regularly. Sometimes I would go there two or three times in a week. At one point, the orphanage became my second home. If I went two days without seeing the children, my mind wouldn't be at rest. I would fret and wonder how they were doing. All kinds of questions would run through my mind: *What is happening? What are they doing? How is that child's fever? Have they had anything to eat?*

A nurse and a caregiver were working in the orphanage, and there was also a resident carpenter. My friend had everything that was needed to make the orphanage work, but it wasn't working.

Building a Case

I wasn't the only one who had grave concerns about the children in the orphanage. Unknown to me, a neighbour who was a lawyer by training had been watching the orphanage. He had surveillance cameras and was also taking notes ...

This man – let's call him John – had been concerned about the children in the orphanage for a while. But when my friend went to America for three months to fundraise and left the children and staff without any means of supporting themselves, he was alarmed. His house was on a hill, right next to the orphanage. Looking from his bedroom window, he could see all kinds of things. Then he started hearing stories from those working in the orphanage.

He heard how the staff felt neglected and abandoned. The director had travelled to America. Jos was in the middle of a crisis (ethnic and religious conflict has reared its ugly head again, so the state was on lockdown), and they had no means of buying food and other things for the children. In addition, the staff members were not being paid. But John knew the orphanage was funded by the highest-ranking AIDS research institute in Nigeria. Where had the money gone?

John started his own investigation. As a lawyer, he knew the value of evidence. So he started filming the goings-on in the orphanage from his house. Sometimes he would go over and find that they didn't have any food or had run out of nappies. There were about five toddlers in the orphanage, so you can imagine what that was like. John bought them nappies and also sanitary towels for the teenage girls. He would even buy soap so they could wash themselves. All the time, John was gradually collecting facts and filming everyone who visited the orphanage ...

People like me.

And I didn't know.

My friend's husband was an elderly man who was rather ill. He didn't go with her to the USA. He seemed to have developed an obsession with one of the teenage girls in the orphanage and would take pictures of her naked in various poses. Everyone at the orphanage knew this, but no one did anything. In fact, one of the boys working there transferred the images to a memory stick. Then he would wave the memory stick in front of the husband and extract whatever he wanted from the old man. So, yes, there was blackmail in the orphanage as well.

John and I weren't the only people to be concerned about the orphanage. Everyone knew that the director was not around. So the community would come with food and necessary things. But as I said, it was a time of crisis. The curfew imposed on Jos lasted about three months, and my friend was away for four. There was only so much people could do.

John, the lawyer, was a devout Christian. He was not married and so could not take the children himself. So he set about trying to find other ways of helping the children. He started writing proposals to charitable organizations to see if they could help. While doing this, his mind constantly turned to "Mummy Bishop" and my regular visits to the orphanage. Later he would say he called me that because the children called me "Mummy" whenever I went to see them, he started thinking that perhaps I would be able to help ...

When he had enough information to indict the orphanage, John went to the police and also reported his findings to the orphanage's donor. I don't know how this happened, but somehow news about what was going on reached America. The next thing we knew, a driver arrived to take the kids. He managed to sneak away with some of them in what amounted to a kidnapping. But when he came back for the last batch, about ten children ranging in age from a few months old to sixteen years, John showed up and threatened criminal action if he took them. So the driver left without taking the children.

But what to do with the children that were left?

12

THE ASSASSINS COME

While all this was going on, a Danish newspaper published a cartoon that was offensive to Muslims and riots broke out in Jos. I find it a bit difficult to talk about what happened, so I will leave it to others to tell you about it before I tell you my side of the story.

Rinji

It was the middle of the night. I looked out the window of the room and saw that our house was surrounded by about thirty armed men. Initially, I thought they were robbers. But there were way too many of them for a robbery. I went to Mum and told her to hide, but she decided to argue with me, right there in my room, which was infuriating. I was nineteen years old, and as Dad wasn't home, I saw myself as the man of the house, responsible for Mum and the other five children in the house.

We started calling everyone we knew to tell them what was happening. Dad was in England at a speaking event, and I couldn't get hold of him. So I called my sister Hannatu, who was studying in Ukraine, and told her to try and call Dad to tell him what was happening. I thought she would have a much better chance of getting through as they were both in Europe.

Then we heard the men coming up the stairs. They burst into my room and demanded to know where the "Chairman" was. I told them I didn't know any such person. Then one of them said, "Bishop Kwashi. We are looking for Bishop Kwashi."

"Oh, sorry, he is not here."

I had barely finished speaking before one of them came at me and gun-butted me. I pretended to black out to give my mum and my younger brother, who had come into the room, more time to get away. I heard my mother shriek, and that was the end of it. Then I really did black out.

When I came to, I heard screaming coming from my parents' bedroom. I could also hear a dull thudding, like someone's head being hit on the wall or the floor. I just felt helpless. My mother was being butchered. My father was away, and there was I, the man of the house, powerless to do anything because two gun-toting men were standing over me and my six-year-old brother.

I could hear everything that was going on. There was the sound of a bottle breaking, like it was being broken on someone's head. And still, I couldn't do anything. My imagination ran wild, and all I could think of was my mother. My helplessness and the knowledge that we were at the attackers' mercy was the worst. It was as if time stood still. A second was like an hour, and all I could hear was my mother's screams.

I heard a click and I thought, *They have killed my mother ...*

I screamed at the guard, "What have you done to my mum?"

My younger brother, Nanminen, who was in the room with me, started hitting and biting the guards. It was ridiculous, because he was only six years old, but I was so proud of him. Then they gun-butted him so hard that they broke his jaw.

Fortunately, all the other children made sure to stay hidden in their rooms when they heard the noise and commotion.

I have no idea at all of how long this went on. All I know is that when the attackers left with my mum, I started calling people again for help.

In the morning, there were many people in the house. They commiserated with us, but I didn't believe them. They were so fake. All I could think was, *Where were you when we needed you yesterday? Where were you when my mother was being butchered? Where were you all?*

I remember some big-shot guy came to see us. He stood proud as a peacock and told us who he was.

"I'm very happy for you," I told him.

He was so surprised at my cheek. But I didn't care. Where were all these people when my mum, my brother and I needed them?

For a long time after that, I really wanted to find the men who attacked my mum. It's only recently that I have let it go. But letting it go doesn't mean that I don't want to see them. I want to put a face to the person who ordered them to do these things to my mother.

Susan Essam

At the time of the attack, I was the bishop's administrative chaplain and lived at the diocesan office. I was woken some time after 3 a.m. by a noise at the gate and the dogs' barking. I heard Gloria's voice.

"Hang on while I get the key," I said in all innocence.

When I opened the gate, I saw two men with guns pointed at me.

It's funny how you don't know how you are going to react until these things happen to you. I just grabbed one of the guns and pointed it up, so it wasn't pointing at me. But I had my torch in my other hand, so I couldn't grab both guns. I thought, *What else can I do?* So I shone my torch full in their faces.

For one awful moment, I thought, *Is this really Mrs Kwashi? Or is it somebody sort of made up to look like Mrs Kwashi, and I have made the most horrendous mistake opening the door?*

She had on a wrapper, and that was it. She was also obviously their hostage.

We were marched into the bishop's office. The men started demanding money. Not just any money. They wanted sterling or dollars or something very valuable.

They gun-butted me across the face so hard that my glasses flew off into a corner somewhere. I said to them, "Look, if you really want me to help you, I need my glasses so I can see. Would you mind letting me get them off the floor?" So they looked for my glasses and gave them to me.

Of course, the frames were so badly bent that they weren't really much use. But I was very careful to be very polite, because my one conscious aim was to just cool everything down, to have complete control. I was on automatic pilot. Really, I was. Nobody shouted or screamed or anything. It was all rather civilized.

We seldom have much money in the office, but that day we did have about £1,000 there. I gave it to them.

Through a small window at the back of the bishop's office, a guy called to the men inside and said, "Time." Mrs Kwashi and I were told to lie down. Then the men went out, and eventually the dogs stopped barking. So I thought, "*Ah ha, that means I can move.*"

It wasn't light yet. It was pitch dark in the bishop's office. But I managed to make my way to the desk without knocking into anything. In those days we had landline phones. By the grace of God it worked. So I felt the keypad, dialled the number of the cathedral, and got straight through to them, "We need help," I said. "We've had armed robbers here."

"You as well?" they said. "So has the bishop's house!"

Then I began to put two and two together. They asked me where Mrs Kwashi was, and I told them she was with me at the diocesan office. They came with police cars, and she was taken to hospital.

Ben

Gloria amazes me with her strength. After the attack, when she was in hospital, she opened her eyes on the second day and noticed that she was the only person in the ward with a mosquito net. She called me closer.

"Ben, can you withdraw some money from my account and buy treated mosquito nets – they're about 1,000 naira apiece – for every patient in this hospital, please?"

I couldn't believe it. She had been badly beaten and yet in her pain she was still thinking of others. The chief medical director of the hospital couldn't believe it either. He invited the media to witness Gloria's donation to the hospital.

Gloria didn't stop there. When she was discharged, she bought over 100,000 naira (about US$500) worth of mosquito nets and went to the villages to distribute them.

But then something else started happening. She began to find that she couldn't see clearly. So she started asking for help with her driving and all that. By the fifth week after the attack, she was blind in both eyes.

The doctors explained that the massive trauma to the back of her head had affected her vision. But her optic nerve was not damaged. We had to go to America for surgery, but thankfully Gloria's sight could be restored.

Whoever sent those people meant to silence me, but it didn't work. Because when Gloria recovered, I became even crazier – more intolerant of injustice in any shape or form. Having been a victim myself, my need to speak out is even more urgent.

Gloria

Sometimes we have a defining moment in our life, and we think, *I'm never taking my life for granted again.* But then the memory of that defining moment fades, and we go back to living the way we used to live.

In my case, I had a defining – well, terrifying – three-and-a-half hour ordeal that literally changed my life and the way I view my time on earth. As a result, I am now more than ever convinced that our time on earth is short. So I am determined to do all that I am physically capable of doing to live out the rest of my days serving Jesus and letting my work and my life reflect his glory. This is not because I think highly of myself but because I want the world to know about his saving grace.

That day in February 2006 had been a busy one. We had just moved into a different house that we had chosen because it was large enough for us to be able to host visitors and minister the gospel. The house has two floors. Our bedrooms are upstairs, and so was a little family parlour where we usually congregated in the evening to talk about our day. From our bedroom, Ben and I had a commanding view of our compound from the front gates all the way to the front door.

We turned on the generator that evening because the power was off. All the family joined in the task of making communion wafers: preparing the mix, putting it in the machine, cutting the wafers, waiting for them to cool down, and then packaging them for customers. All in all, it was a normal day.

Ben was away. He had just been made the international chairman of the Anglican organization known as SOMA (Sharing of Ministries Abroad), and he had gone to England for the official handing over ceremony. You can tell when Ben is not at home because the house is less lively, but I find I get a lot more done around the house!

Ben called at midnight to tell me that he was coming back a day later than planned, which I was really unhappy about. He was due back the following day, Friday, as he was officiating at the wedding of one of his pastors that Saturday. The wedding had already been postponed twice, and here Ben was telling me to ask another of our pastors to officiate. I told him off. He grovelled. We made up, and I went to bed.

About 1:30 a.m. I was woken by voices and some pounding, as if someone was being beaten. I got out of bed, peeped through the window, and saw our security guard being pulled towards our front door. He had been severely beaten up. There were about thirty men surrounding the house. Some were wearing jeans, others kaftans. They were all carrying machetes and knives.

I was gripped by a cold fear. *Who were these people*, I thought, and *who can we call for help?* I went to Rinji's room. He was also awake. We both looked out of the window. When the men saw us, they called out and told us not to bother phoning the police, as we weren't going to receive any help from them, nor from anyone else. They were right. We tried calling people, but none of our calls went through.

Rinji and I started discussing what to do. He insisted that I go back to my bedroom to hide, but I refused. I knew what he was trying to do, but I wasn't having it. I am a mother, and my place is with my children. By this time, Nanminen had also come into the room. We prayed, asking God for protection and guidance for what to do next. When he finished praying, Rinji tried phoning his older sister, Hannatu, who was living and studying in the Ukraine. Strangely enough, that call went through. He told her what was happening, and she called her father in the UK who started calling people in Nigeria for help.

After the phone call, Rinji and I carried on with our debate about where to hide. This was about forty minutes after we first spotted the unwanted visitors through our windows. By this time, they had broken all the windows but couldn't get in because the windows were protected by sturdy iron burglar bars. Then we heard a squeak. I knew that squeak. It came from one of the back doors. Someone had left the key hanging there and the men had been able to enter the house.

They found me in Rinji's room.

I asked who they were and what they wanted. They shouted at the three of us, "Where is Bishop Kwashi? Where is the chairman of the Christian Association of Nigeria?" Rinji told them that the bishop wasn't at home. They gun-butted him unconscious, held his younger brother hostage and dragged me to my room.

When we were in my room, they started hitting me on the head and taking turns hitting me all over.

"Where is CAN?"

Whack! On my head.

"Where is the bishop?"

Whack!

"We know he was meant to come back today. Stop lying!"

Whack! Whack! Whack!

They didn't give me a chance to answer.

Thud!

One of them broke a bottle over my head. Blood spurted into my eyes.

"If you don't tell us where the bishop is, we'll 'waste' you with our guns."

The beating continued.

The assassins were so confident Ben was back in Jos and hiding in the house that I knew these weren't run-of-the-mill armed robbers – we have plenty of those in Nigeria. These were more like assassins sent to silence my husband. Because of the way they spoke and kept on calling my husband "CAN", I also knew that whoever sent them had a grudge against Ben's preaching.

One of them cocked his gun to shoot me, but their leader ordered that I be stripped. I was held down by four of them and spread-eagled. They stuffed the broken edge of the bottle into me, and as I lay there screaming, they took the wooden end of a mop, rammed it in into me and kept turning it. I have never experienced such agony in my life! I screamed and prayed for Jesus to help me.

My attackers were all young men. They didn't bother to cover their faces, nor the delight they took in violating my body. I prayed for my six-year-old son, Nanminen, and for Rinji – he was out cold on the floor when they took me to my room. I didn't know what had happened to them. I prayed to God for help – for someone to help us, to protect my children and my foster-children, and to stop this agony I was going through.

As this was going on, the men were debating whether the bishop was hiding in the house, and if he was, where was he most likely to hide? If he really wasn't there, they were planning to leave me dead so the bishop would have to deal with the grief and misery of finding a dead wife on his arrival home from the UK. But after a while, they decided they would go to the diocesan office about a twenty-minute walk away. I'm not sure why. Perhaps they thought they would find the bishop there. Or maybe they thought they could get their hands on some money. I really don't know.

I passed out. While I was out cold, the assassins ransacked the house looking for the bishop. When they couldn't find him, they came back to the bedroom and dragged me naked downstairs and outside the house.

I came to as I was being dragged down the stairs. When I breathed in the fresh air, I asked Jesus to give me strength. Strength came! I asked the men to give me something to cover my naked body. They agreed and gave me a wrapper, which they got from somewhere in the house. Then they placed a carton of soft drinks on my head and told me to lead them to the diocesan office.

All in all, the assassins had been in the house for about two-and-a-half hours.

I was bleeding and so dizzy that I could barely see where I was going. But God was my strength. He enabled me to walk the 2.5 kilometres (1.5 miles) to the office. As we walked, the attackers talked and laughed and helped themselves to the soft drinks I was carrying on my head.

One of the attackers was a young man who kept calling me "Mama". I staggered, lost my way and fell a few times, as I couldn't really see where I was going. But this boy would help me up with a combination of urging and threats.

"Mama, if you don't keep up, you will be killed," he said.

"Mama, we know he is back. Just tell us where the bishop is."

"Mama, are you really willing to die for this man? Why don't you just tell us where he is?"

I had many thoughts going through my head. I think my overriding thought was that I did not know what the end result of all this would be. But all through the experience, I chose to persevere and to keep praying to Jesus. I had absolute confidence in his saving power – whatever the end result would be.

When we arrived at the diocesan office, I called out to Susan, the diocese administrator, to open the gates. I heard the attackers talking about physically assaulting her. But I reminded them that they had said they were only interested in the bishop and me and that no one else would be hurt.

Susan opened up the gates and was immediately taken hostage. When they led us into the office, I fainted. The next thing I remember was opening up my eyes and seeing the doctor. I was in hospital. Apparently, I had been in hospital for six hours before opening my eyes. But I was so thankful to be alive!

When I saw my husband and children for the first time, more than anything else, I was just thankful that everybody was safe and well. I told Ben that I would rather have him alive than be a widow. As I was speaking to him, I noticed that I was the only patient in the ward who had a mosquito net.

That didn't sit well with me at all. I asked Ben to withdraw some money from my account and make sure that everyone else in the hospital had a mosquito net.

I was in hospital for a week before I was discharged, and was just so grateful to have Ben around. He ran all over the place to make sure I was okay.

As soon as I started feeling better, life started coming back to normal. However, my sight started failing, and within five weeks of the attack, I went blind. That was a far bigger issue than my emotions. I started to think about what to spend the rest of my life doing, and doing it fast because I had no more time to waste.

I have experienced how very transient this life is. I live with the reminder that it is very short. I am moved by the fact that the young men who carried out these evil acts are also children with mothers. As far as I'm concerned, this fact calls for positive action to help mothers raise God-fearing children so that there will be no room for those who want to recruit young minds for evil. This is the urgency I feel about preaching the gospel to youth and children.

I didn't know that I was going to be tested again, that the assassins would come back just over a year later. And this time, my husband would be at home.

Early days: A few more children added to the family

13

THE LADY IN THE RED VAN

Roughly a year after that assault, matters came to a head at the orphanage. John, the lawyer, reported the situation to the police, and also notified the orphanage's main sponsor in Abuja about what was going on. That organization immediately sent some of its staff to investigate and they decided that they needed to remove the children from the orphanage. But they didn't know where to put them. They tried several organizations. Some were willing to take two, or at most three children, but not all ten of them. Others just didn't have the space for any more children.

While all this was going on, John suddenly remembered "Mummy Bishop", the lady in the red van who regularly came to visit the children. He knew that I cared for the children and, equally, that they loved me. That was clear to everyone from the film footage he had of me visiting the children and their happy faces every time I came to see to them.

"She's the bishop's wife and our last hope. Why don't we try her?" he said.

The donor's staff went to Ben's office and told him about the situation. I was asked to come to the office too.

When I arrived, we went into the chapel, and they began to talk. I think they thought they were trying to talk me to into accepting responsibility for the children. They mentioned money – "We know you can help, and we will help you with money" and all that. But really, they were wasting their breath because my mind was made up. I didn't care about the money. These were children who I knew and had been visiting in the orphanage for a long while. I knew their names and their needs. The world might call them orphans, but as far as I was concerned, in my heart they were already my children. So I didn't have to think twice when I gave them my answer.

"Yes, I'll take them."

There was no way I could tell them to come back in a week, while I thought about what to do. The children needed somewhere to stay, and fast. I had to act quickly.

Fortunately we still had our old home on Argak Close, despite having moved to the new house in which we were attacked. The donor's staff came with me to look at it. They needed to give it their approval because, according to the law, they were now the legal guardians of the children.

After that, we went to the orphanage. There was only one woman there who was looking after all the children. Everyone else had gone. I could see that she wanted to flee the orphanage too, but didn't have the heart to leave the children by themselves. Yet in her heart of hearts, she had already left. It was only her body that was there with the children. When she was told that they were handing over the children's care to me, she said, "Okay. Ah, they are very happy." She left a week after we moved all the children to my old house in Argak Close, saying, "You are a good woman. I'm not like you. I can't stay here with these children. One day, I'll be like you. But not just yet."

The donor's staff tried to introduce me to the children. But the children said, "Oh, we already know who she is. She's Mummy Bishop!"

"Well, things are different now," the donor's staff said. "Now, she is going to be your mother forever."

Then we started packing up everything because we had to vacate the premises – not least because even the rent had expired. (I later paid the landlord the remainder of the rent, and was refunded by the donor organization.)

The packing didn't go well. In his haste to take that all he could in the short time he had available, the driver (the same one who had once tried to take the children away) seemed to be more interested in stealing than in packing. He took the leg of a chair, a broken table or whatever he could quickly lay his hands on. So there wasn't much left that we could use.

There were a lot of toys, gifts from donors and well-wishers, but most of them were broken. There has been no supervision of the children and their play had been destructive.

Other stuff was so soiled with faeces and dirt that we had to burn it, particularly as many of the children were HIV-positive.

In the end, we couldn't take anything of worth with us from the orphanage to Argak Close. What little we did take, I put in storage because I don't want anyone to accuse me of stealing stuff that belong to them.

St John's College kindly lent us their bus, and we loaded the children into it and took them to Argak Close. There wasn't time to do anything much before they arrived. We simply swept the house and laid down mats we'd hastily bought from the market. We didn't even have cooking pots.

But despite lacking so much, the children were happy. They were delighted to leave the orphanage.

Life at Argak Close

Things were really hectic for the first few days, and the donor's staff were not particularly helpful. They were used to a bureaucracy. They told me I had to draw up a list of things that I needed and determine how much they would cost before they could give me the money to buy them. But between running around trying to get anti-retroviral drugs for the HIV-positive children, cleaning up faeces after the other children, cooking, cleaning, and trying to make sure the autistic children were okay, I had neither the time nor the inclination to make a list. I was flying by the seat of my pants and responding to the children's needs as they emerged. Besides, the kind of financial and organizational accountability they were asking from me, with all the paperwork involved, was too much to contemplate.

I was a novice at this. Half of the time, I didn't even know what I was doing. I was just living day to day, responding to the needs of the children. And here were the donor's staff, asking me to write stupid lists and to make sure I "costed" everything correctly. If only they had just said, "Look, we know that you need these things – this is what we used to give the woman who used to run the orphanage. How about we give you one-tenth of that and save us all some paperwork?" Or, "She used to get x and y on a regular basis. So, you can have the same." That would have made my life so much easier. But instead, they were asking me for receipts for everything. But that's by the by. This was God's venture, and I had better things to do with my time than fill out forms. (Needless to say, in everything we did we tried to be accountable and to have receipts. I became a receipt person overnight. But some things like feeding were difficult to receipt at short notice.)

After about three days, Ben raised enough money from the church to buy mattresses for everyone. Later, I got some pots. One of the older boys from the orphanage, Zakaria, who was about fourteen, helped me with the cooking. So did women from the Mothers' Union once the news got around that Mummy Bishop had been "given" some children.

Gloria and Ben cooking lunch for the children of Zambiri
in the morning before going to the office

The days and months that followed passed in a daze. I would wake up and leave my house and go to Argak Close. I would spend the day there, often not coming back to my home before 9:00 p.m., or sometimes even 11:00 p.m.

I spent a lot of time at the other house with the children because I really wanted them to feel that they were in a secure home with their mother.

Much of the time, I was so busy that I forgot to eat. Late at night, I would come back to my own home and find that someone had put something aside for me, and I would think, *Gosh, I haven't eaten today.* Sometimes I would get home and there wouldn't be anything, and I would start scavenging for food.

Meanwhile my own children at home would joke, "Mummy, you have abandoned us."

I would tell them, "You have always had me. All you have to do is open up the fridge, and you can feed yourself. These children can't do that. They are severely traumatized. They need me."

But the children's problems were not just the results of the trauma. I had to start from scratch to teach them how to behave and take care of themselves. Some were autistic, others were HIV-positive. But the ones who didn't have medical or other issues still had to be taken care of, because it was very easy for them to fall through the cracks. I had to teach them all how to bathe properly, how to brush their teeth, to stop destroying toys and not to pee on themselves. Those first months at Argak Close I felt as if I was running a psychiatric home!

Four months after we moved the children from the orphanage to Argak Close, my younger brother Thomas came from Numan to see us and was told that I was in Argak Close. He hurried there. He and my uncle, my father's younger brother, found me there. Thomas later told me that he cried from the time he left Argak Close to the time he went back to Numan. He didn't sleep for three days. On the third day, he called me.

"You're not doing this alone. My wife, Miriam, and I are moving to Jos to help you."

His call was an answer to prayer, because I had been wondering just how long I could carry on doing this alone. Sometimes I arrived at Argak Close at five in the morning because I wanted to do morning devotions with the children, and I didn't want them to wake up and not find me around. In fact, many people thought I had moved into Argak Close, but I hadn't. I was going to and from my house. At night, I wanted to be there when the children closed their eyes, and I would hang around just to make sure I was there if they needed me. There was so much to do.

After Thomas and his wife, Miriam, came to help me, we also started looking for someone else to help us. We wanted a retired, motherly figure who would live with the children in Argak Close. I didn't want someone of working age, because caring for the children would seem like a job to them. I wanted someone who was retired, who had time on her hands, who had raised children herself and knew what it was like to be a mother. I also wanted someone who had a specific calling to work with orphans. We eventually found someone, but she wasn't keen to live with the children. So she would come first thing in the morning and leave at night.

But she wasn't always much help. We were trying to potty train some of the younger children. We would tell them, "If you need to poo, say 'Poo', and we will take you to the toilet." But the old woman didn't follow through. She would stand and watch as the children peed and pooed on themselves and did not tell them off. If I spanked the children, she would cry.

Finally, I told her straight: "Mama, I don't think you can do this work. It's not like I don't love these children – they are mine. But if I didn't tolerate such behaviour from the children I carried in my womb, why should I tolerate it from these whom I also profess to be mine?"

"Mummy Bishop, these children don't have anybody ..." she said.

"They do. I am their mother. And I am teaching them values. Am I supposed to sit back and watch as they pee and poo on themselves until they are ten years old?"

It was a bit of a struggle with the old woman. So I started thinking of other ways to get helpers. Some young people came to help. At one point, we had about twenty young volunteers from church. But in time, they faded away to school and other things.

The donor told us to look for workers to help with recreation, which I did. They were paid for about six months, and then the funding stopped. When I pressed the donor for payment, they would tell me they hadn't received our grant report or application. Or perhaps it had got lost in the mail. Or they said that I should apply for this category in that district. Then I would start the whole process over again. I had to tell the workers that I didn't have any money to pay them because the donor wasn't giving us any funding.

By this time, I was getting really fed up with the paperwork. I thought, *Am I doing this for people or for God? The donor's staff don't know when I take these children to hospital in the middle of the night. They are not around when I leave my house at 4:30 in the morning and drive to Argak Close to make sure I'm there when the children wake up so I can do their devotions with them. They are making this feel like work, and as far as I'm concerned, it's not. It's a ministry.*

So I called a meeting and asked the donor to formally sign over the care of the children to me, which they were happy to do – it gave them one less thing to worry about. The only thing they insisted on was that I formally set up a charitable organization, which they helped me to do.

After that, I could breathe. My children were now formally mine. Their last names became Kwashi, and I could raise them with all the care and love that God had put in my heart for them – without interference from anyone and without feeling beholden to some organization just because they were funding us.

So that was that. However, there was still the fact that I was running two homes. In the morning, I would wake up and run to Argak Close, sometimes without bathing, and my sister-in-law Miriam would tell me what the children had been saying or doing.

"This one said that he was in a cult. We haven't slept all night."

"This one did this to that one, and we've tried to settle the dispute. But it's still ongoing."

"This one was sick all night. And that one just threw up blood."

I would then stand and think, *Lord, which one should I take to which specialist hospital first?*

My head constantly felt like it was going to explode. Sometimes, I would question myself and pray, *Lord, are these really children or psychiatric cases? Have you really called me to do this?*

I didn't want to make the same mistakes that my friend had made, the kind of mistakes that resulted in neglected children. But I knew I was heading in that direction. There was so much to do, and I could only keep track of so many things.

Besides, I couldn't keep friends or focus on one thing. If I was in my home, I would be thinking of the children in Argak Close. If I was in Argak Close, I would be thinking of my other home and my church work and also trying to deal with the crises in Argak Close, of which there were many every day.

Those six months were tough. Two days were like ten days. When I think back, I don't honestly know how I managed. I was angry a lot of the time, from exhaustion and mental fatigue, and I took my anger out on everyone, especially the workers.

"Why have you done this?" I would say. "I thought you loved these children like your own ..."

Every night when I came back from Argak Close, I would pour out my frustration to Ben, and he would get frustrated too. So one day I just said, "Honestly, let's just bring these children to live with us, because what's the point of keeping two houses?"

Fortunately, it took a while to get to this point, for I would never have wanted those children to have to endure the second attack on our family.

14

THE ASSASSINS RETURN

I have been talking about how hard things were with all the orphans. But there were good times too. There were nights I spent at home. One of them in August 2007 was particularly good. As we retired to bed, we teased Ben because he was wearing the cassock of the Egyptian Church. I had no concerns. I had all my children with me. The house was joyful, so lively that day. We finished our normal night prayer and wished each other goodnight.

About 2:00 a.m., I heard a noise. My heart started thudding. When I looked out of the window, my heart sank. I prayed, *Not again, Lord.*

The children heard what was going on. Rinji went to the window. So did Becky, the children's nanny and caretaker, and Jacob, Ben's brother.

There were about thirty men outside. This time, they had come prepared. They had machetes, pickaxes, sledgehammers and rocks. Because of what had happened before, we had installed a steel front door and interior steel doors in other strategic areas of the house. But these guys knew what they were doing. It was clear that they were on a mission and wouldn't stop until they got what they came for: Ben.

Boom. Boom. The attackers kept hitting the same area of the front door to weaken it and break it down.

We tried to pray, but it was hard. All I could hear was the *boom, boom, boom* as the men tried to break down the door. I could also hear their voices. "Open this door, right now!"

Wham! Boom!

These were very strong men.

I recognized some of their voices from the last time. It was the same men.

Ben stood up and said, "God, if this is my last day, just take me home. But don't let anyone else be hurt."

I told Ben to be quiet. "No, who told you that it's your last day? And if you think I'm raising these kids myself, you have another think coming!"

You see, even in the midst of danger, we still retained our sense of humour.

"Gloria, if this is anything like the last time, then they are on a mission. They won't rest until they get who they're coming for: me. I have nowhere to run to. It's in God's hands."

All I could think of was how short life is. Here one day, gone the next.

Ben kept trying to get through to someone on the telephone. He knew a lot of people. He had been in the army as a young man, and many of his army friends were now generals and whatnot. He called a particular friend who was high up in the Nigerian army. I could hear both sides of the conversation.

"They have come for me. They have found me at home," Ben said.

"I can hear the noise, Ben. I promise you that nothing will happen. Get off the phone and leave it with me."

Click. The phone disconnected.

Ben went to the window.

"Sit down," he said.

"I will not sit down." I could see from the look on his face that he wanted to tell me not to worry, that if anything happened to him, the kids and I would be well taken care of. But I wasn't having it. "I'm not looking after these children alone! I won't, you hear me? I won't!"

Ben tried other numbers, but no calls went through. We tried my mobile; the same thing happened. Everyone in the house was calling, but there was no network. We just couldn't get through.

"What are we going to do?" I asked. "Perhaps we should hide under the bed."

I don't know what I was thinking. All I knew was that if those men found Ben at home, they would definitely kill him. I knew about assassinations. I also knew from experience how people who are being attacked call for help, but usually none came.

"Ben, you can't ... if you die ..." I could barely get the words out of my mouth.

"Look, if it is my time, my prayer is that none of you will be hurt."

We started calling everyone we knew again: police, whoever. But the calls just weren't getting through.

Ben sat on the bed and we heard *Wham!* The door was giving way. That door was bullet proof. Someone must have told them about it, and they had come with the equipment to take it out.

Boom! The steel door caved in, and we heard the men run up the stairs. Everyone ran to their respective rooms. After that there was silence, or to put it bluntly, a terrifying wait to see how things would unfold.

I couldn't look at my husband. I didn't know what was happening in the children's bedrooms. This drama was Ben's and mine.

I ran from our bedroom to the bathroom and turned on the lights. I hoped that the assassins would know that our neighbours could see the lights, and perhaps they would stop.

They came straight up the stairs.

One group went to Rinji's room. The whole house was silent – the kind of silence that waits for evil to unleash its terrible deeds on God's children.

When they went into Becky's room, they started pushing and shoving her. She told them to leave her alone.

"Where is your telephone? You people were phoning, you were phoning the police," they shouted at her.

"No, I didn't phone."

"Where is your mobile phone?!"

Becky is so clever. She had put her mobile phone in her underwear. But if it had rung, God knows what would have happened.

The men who had gone into Rinji's room started beating him. He said he felt in his heart that he shouldn't fight back, so he didn't. He lay there while they rained blows on him. They didn't spare Nanminen, my youngest son either, even though he was only seven.

For me, time stood still. I had a vague recollection of my children and prayed that they wouldn't be hurt. But in such a situation, everything is about you. The pain, everything you are going through ...

I turned off the bathroom light, but left the door slightly ajar. Cowering there, I watched as four or five men entered our bedroom.

My husband just stood there, quiet. He was wearing the white cassock that we had been making fun of a few hours back. I think a bishop from Egypt or somewhere had given it to him. It's a bit like a maternity gown and has a rope that ties it together, like the clothes people wear in the Jesus films.

As Ben stood in the bedroom waiting for the men, I could see that he was ready to die. He looked like a man who knew that his last minutes were upon him. I kept watching and praying that John, our army friend, had been able to get help. Then I panicked and thought, *What if John decides to call us back and the phone rings? The men will hear it!*

I dropped my mobile into a bucket of water in the bath. I thought that even if they found me and took my phone, it would be waterlogged and completely useless to them. Then I stood still, not knowing what to do.

I heard them say, "Man of God, we have come for you."

I just heard my husband say, "Mm-nn."

They grabbed Ben and dragged him out of the room, past the bathroom where I was hiding, and down the corridor.

I was shaking and praying, "Lord, if they're taking him away and there's not going to be bloodshed, then what are they going to do? We've had enough bloodshed in this house, Lord. Whatever we have done, have mercy on us. I don't know what we have done to cause this, but have mercy on us."

I kept praying, hoping that the assassins would not remember that Ben's wife was around. Or maybe because they already had Ben, the one they had come for, they wouldn't really care about me.

I don't know how long I stood there in the bathroom, hoping and praying. Whether it was five minutes or more, I cannot really tell. Sometimes you don't know how long something has taken. Yes, everything is just ... Sometimes things are happening too fast. Other times, we cannot really explain. So I waited there.

I reached out to retrieve the mobile from the pail of water to try and call someone again. As I was trying, the bucket moved. I heard the assassins coming back. Someone tried to push open the door of the room next to the bathroom, which we use as a storage room of sorts. There was a lot of junk in there, so the door was quite difficult to open.

I cowered behind the bathroom door as the men dragged Ben back into the small parlour off our bedroom. I didn't know whether to say "Thank you, Lord" or what. I was just blank, but very, very scared.

I could hear the men talking, but I couldn't make out what they were saying. Then I clearly heard Ben say, "Please let me pray."

I peered through a crack in the door and saw Ben kneel and then prostrate himself. I think Ben had a Bible in his hand, I didn't hear a gunshot, and I didn't hear any kind of ... I didn't hear anything.

Someone wandered into the bathroom. He shone a torch in my eyes. I was dazzled by the light and couldn't see anything. But I could hear my heart racing!

I heard the guy say, "Eh, so his wife is here!"

To me he said, "Come out here, come out."

I came out and *whack!* on my behind with a gun. Then I really thanked God for my big behind. Without it, that assassin would have hit my spinal cord, and where would I be? If these people hadn't killed me, they would definitely have paralysed me.

The guy kept on hitting my behind with his gun. It was painful.

"Stop hitting me," I told him. I don't know where I got the courage to even speak to him.

"Shut up. Where is your telephone? You have two telephones," he said.

"Me?"

"Yes, you have two mobiles."

Whether he was guessing or what, I don't know.

"Okay, true. I have two telephones." However, one was no good, so I kept it in one of the wardrobe drawers.

The man followed me into the bedroom and kept on pushing and whacking my behind and back with his gun. As I went into the room, I saw Ben's Blackberry lying there on the floor. Despite all my fear and confusion, I was still able to think quickly enough to nudge the Blackberry under the bed with my foot. Then I went to the wardrobe and started pulling out the drawers, pretending to look for my mobile.

"Quick!" He hit me again. "Quickly. Bring it quickly!"

"I'm looking for it. I don't know where the phone is kept," I said. "I'm looking for it."

Then I turned back to the drawers. I brought out the dead handset and gave it to him.

"Where is the other one?"

I said, "It's in the toilet."

The man pushed me towards the bathroom again, still hitting me with his gun. We moved past Ben, who was lying prostrate on the parlour floor with his Bible open in front of him. The Lord only knew what he was reading.

Later Ben told me that he had taken that position so that if they shot him, he would die quickly. Apparently, the men had told him that they were bringing him back to our small parlour because they wanted to shoot him in front of me once they had found me.

As I retrieved my mobile from the bucket of water I had thrown it into, the man hit me again.

"You are evil!" he said. "You threw a perfectly good mobile into water!"

I started arguing with him. "Did you see me do such a thing?"

He ignored me, pocketed my mobile and left me in the bathroom.

Next door, one of the men was rifling through our storage room. Then I heard another one of them come and scold him. "Come on, drop this! Drop this thing and get out now!"

I heard some movement. Then doors opened and closed. The house became quiet.

Slowly I tiptoed out of the bathroom and into our sitting room. My husband was still prostrate on the floor. He was still alive, and was mumbling something as if he was praying. I knelt down and took his hand to see if it was still warm.

"Are they gone?" he asked.

I said, "Yes, they have gone."

We held hands. I heard someone come into the room. It was Rinji. All three of us held hands and began to pray. Then we got up. As we did, other people joined us.

Someone went to wake up Hannatu. "What's going on? What happened?" she asked.

She hadn't heard a thing!

We all laughed.

I think God injected Hannatu with Valium from heaven! The men hadn't even found her room or anything, for which I thank God. At the sight of them, she would have collapsed! Everybody sat down, and we counted heads. Everybody in the house was alive.

Two and half hours later, we started hearing police sirens and everything.

Then we heard gunshots and *bah-bah-bah-bah* outside. *Bah-bah-bah* with a megaphone. "It's the police. It's the police," came from outside.

They had surrounded the house. *Bah-bah-bah*, "It's the police. It's the police."

We just sat quietly in the house and started singing, praising the Lord, but refused to go out.

They kept calling, "It's the police. Come out, it's the police."

What was the point of going out to meet them? The gates were wide open. The front door had been broken down. So why were they saying that whoever was in the house should come out? Besides, even if the assassins had still been in the house, really, all the police had to do was storm the building instead of coming two hours after they had left and shouting into the megaphone, "Come out!"

The second visit from the assassins confirmed to me that our security is only in the Lord. During the first visit, I can say that I was scared. Terrified, even. During the second visit, I was also afraid. But the fear was not like the first time, with the anxiety and other things that followed. So now I can say that faith-wise, the second visit really deepened my faith in the Lord.

Also because of the second visit I can now see, truly, that in this life, anything can happen. Things can change in the blink of an eye. You are just doing your thing, you go to bed, and you wake up. Even in waking up, you could meet death that second or later in the day.

Those men were not common thieves. They could have had their pick of anything in the house. But they didn't take anything. They were assassins. And it was the Lord who saved us – and is still keeping us safe. The first time the assassins came, I called the police and tried everything. Nothing worked. But God spared my life. The second time, we again tried everything. We prayed and prayed. They took Ben out and brought him back. But what they said they were going to do, they couldn't do.

Ben's Story

About eighteen months after the first attack, the assassins came back. This time the house was full. Hannatu was home from Ukraine. My younger brother, Jacob, the Bishop of Zonkwa, had come to pick up his son from school in Jos, and he was in Hannatu's room, which was why Hannatu had moved to another room. Rinji was in his room, and the other children were all home as well. The children from the orphanage were in Argak Close, our old house, for which I thank God.

The assassins came with hacksaws, hammers, sledgehammers, ladders and more. There was not going to be any way out. They hacked out our steel door in thirty minutes, and then they were in the house – straight into my bedroom.

When we heard them come in, Gloria went to our bathroom to hide.

They found me in the bedroom on my knees, praying.

Their leader said, "Man of God, it is not time for prayers now."

I said, "Fine."

"We have been assigned to kill you."

I said, "Okay."

"If you have money to give us, we will leave you, and we will tell the people we didn't see you at home."

So I asked them, "How much?"

They said, "Three million naira" (about US$12,000).

"I don't have three million naira. You should have told me yesterday." Even in the midst of what was a delicate situation, I still had my sense of humour.

So they took me downstairs and out into the open field of our gardens. The man whom I think was assigned to kill me was standing there with a knife in one hand and a gun in the other. He was shaking, whether from adrenaline or drugs, I don't know.

Their leader said, "No, we're not going kill him. He's going to give us money."

The guy with the knife and gun said, "No, no, no."

Suddenly, their leader screamed, "No, we changed our minds. Why not do it in his bedroom?"

They took me back upstairs to our bedroom. They didn't touch me or hit me or anything.

I told them, "If you're going to do anything to me, please let me pray."

They said, "Fine."

I was aware that Gloria was still in the bathroom. I picked up my Bible, and then I realized that my reading glasses were on the bedside table. I went and picked them up and started reading from Psalms. I was going to read Psalm 124. But meanwhile, apparently out of fear, I was reciting Psalm 23, because in my heart I was begging God, *Let there be no bloodshed, only mine. Let there be no bloodshed, only mine.*

Psalm 124

1 If the LORD had not been on our side
  let Israel say

2 if the LORD had not been on our side
  when people attacked us,

3 they would have swallowed us alive
  when their anger flared against us;

4 the flood would have engulfed us,
  the torrent would have swept over us,

5 the raging waters
  would have swept us away.

6 Praise be to the LORD,
  who has not let us be torn by their teeth.

7 We have escaped like a bird
  from the fowler's snare;
  the snare has been broken,
  and we have escaped.

8 Our help is in the name of the LORD,
  the Maker of heaven and earth.

Then I prostrated myself on the floor and pleaded with the Lord. I knew they had discovered Gloria in the bathroom, because I heard some movement in that direction. They brought her out and hit her, and then I didn't see Gloria again.

As I lay prostrate on the floor, I heard the men say, "Let's go!" I took that to mean that they were going to ransack the house even more. I didn't look up. Suddenly, I felt Gloria's hands hold me. She said, "Pray, pray."

We held each other and prayed. A little later, Rinji came into our bedroom.

I asked him, "What are you doing here?"

He said, "Daddy, they are gone."

In all, the assassins were in the house for about one hour and forty minutes, far less than the first time.

Several things happened as a result of this second visit of the killers. For one, it has made Hannatu more determined to serve Nigeria. "Daddy, after university, I am coming back to Nigeria. Life or death, we must help the coming generation, we must serve our people," she said.

But Rinji is the one I think is insane! Because after the first incident, he decided to go into ministry. After the second incident, he decided to go to theological college – full-time.

15

BRINGING OUR CHILDREN HOME

After about six months, I made the decision to move the children from our old house in Argak Close so that they could live with us at the mission house. By this time, the number of children had increased from ten to about fifty because we added more children from other run-down orphanages.

Before we did this, I had been running myself ragged. Rising early, I would basically run from my house to the old house where the children were to make sure I did the morning devotions with them, praying that nothing had happened to them in the six or so hours I had been away. My brother's decision to come down and help me with the children was a huge load off my back. I trusted him and his wife implicitly, and I knew they would do a good job. But even so, I was distracted trying to run two households. So one day Ben and I brought all the children to our home, where we now all live together. We laid mats, mattresses and everything else we could find in the guestroom, downstairs in the living room and anywhere else we could for the little ones. They slept head to tail. We temporarily put the older ones in the gatehouse.

In the morning, I woke everyone up.

"You are now living with Mummy and Daddy," I told the children. "After praying, we will set up some ground rules. But first, let's thank God for a good night's sleep ..."

Hannatu's Story

I had known about the children for a long time because mum would tell us about her visits to the orphanage. When she came home, she would say things like, "This is what is happening at that orphanage. John the lawyer says that the kids are being molested … Please pray."

Even when I was studying medicine in Ukraine, mum kept me updated on what was going on. At one point, she moved one of the girls who had been molested at the orphanage into our home so that she could give her the care and attention she needed. I knew what was coming.

I called my father. "Daddy, we're in trouble. You know what Mum's like. This is just the beginning. I think we should just say no."

It wasn't that I didn't want this girl or any of the children living with us, but I know the kind of mother I've got. After moving one child into our home, there was no way she would stop. Inevitably, others would follow.

Mum called me after I had spoken to Dad. She put on what I call her "puppy voice". "Hannatu, there is no hope for these children. They need a place to live. You have already been blessed with two parents. These kids have nothing. And if God has placed them in my path and on my heart, then who am I to say no?"

I called my father again. "Daddy, we're in trouble. She is really going to do it."

When the children were assigned to mum's care, they were moved to our old house about 10 minutes' drive away from where we live now. But this was very tough on mum, trying to manage and meet the needs of the children and her family. She eventually realized that she couldn't carry on like that, which was why she decided to bring all of the children into our home. They are still here today.

I was away in Ukraine when the move took place. But when I came home, it was awful. The stench, I mean, not the children coming. We had to leave the windows open for about six months before people could enter the rooms where the children initially were!

As a medical student, I saw things from a health perspective. I understood that these children came from villages and remote areas where basic hygiene was not an integral part of their daily lives. They had no social skills, etiquette or knowledge of how to live like human beings. They were ignorant about such things. Because they had been so neglected at the orphanage, they had never been taught how to behave.

When mum brought the children to the main house, each room had about seven children. There were so many of them that we just spread them around, as we didn't have enough space. The situation was a medical hazard. The children would pee on the beds and the carpets, and the toilets would overfill with faeces. The children really didn't know how to take care of things, so they would break things like beds and chairs and leave them broken. I would come in, look at the mattresses, peep into the toilet and just pray, Oh God, *help*.

To say this was a period of adjustment is an understatement. I have never resented having the children around because our parents have always taught us that life is about giving, being thankful and being of service. What was hard was educating the children about the value of things and not breaking them; that if you need the loo, go to the toilet instead of peeing on the mattress; that you empty your bowels in the toilet, not around it ... Those kinds of things, and *Stop writing on the walls!*

After the children came, I don't think I ever had my room to myself again. At night, I would find the least full room and just bed down for the night, which was fine with me. To be honest, I don't much like staying in my room by myself because that is so boring. At least with other people in the room, I was never bored. There were always things going on.

So from the beginning, we have always been a part of the children's lives. Mum made sure everyone had a responsibility. For example, the older children (the teenagers) were each assigned a young child to take care of. My mum is a firm believer in every member of the family contributing something to the family. So the older children would bathe the young children, feed them, dress them and just generally be the go-to person for their child. It's a great system, and it works.

Rinji's Story

I had been away somewhere, can't remember where. I came home, and the house was full of children. As the night drew close, I asked my mum how we were going to take them back to Argak Close, and she said, "No, they are staying with us."

I said, "Okay." And that was that.

Every time I travelled and came back, the children would increase in number. At the time I am writing this, I haven't been in Nigeria for a few years, due to health issues. But I know that when I do eventually go back, there will probably be 400 children in the house! It is just the way mum is. She can't stop.

I think that having the children has added a new dynamic to our family. For one, I was vigilant about my personal items. Normal investigations about who nicked my ice cream, which would take a few minutes in a normal home, take a lot longer in ours.

But it's not all bad. Having the children has made life more interesting.

Nendel's Story

I have so much to write about my parents. Because of Mummy's huge heart she has loved and raised so many children as hers. I remember one time she went to a village called Kalep. The situation was really dire in that village. There was no clean water, food was a luxury that many people could ill-afford, and the standard of living was just tough. Seeing a woman giving her child muddy water to drink because there was no clean water was the last straw for Mummy. She had to bring the mother and child to the mission house. They stayed for a while and then went back to the village. We later heard that the boy had died.

As a child, I really struggled about whether to accept the love of my parents, which I saw as hate, or to accept the hate and deceit of others which I saw as love. I never understood that love was when people pointed you in the right direction by disciplining you. Mummy was always around and she never gave us breathing space. I thought that she hated me because she did not give me the freedom I wanted. The devil used that to tie me down to such an extent that I never trusted my parents enough to share my thoughts and feelings with them, or to tell them what was bothering me. I locked up so much hate in my heart! But God has freed me from all that.

Mummy's love does not stop at the level of her family but extends to others as well. She reaches out to others to such an extent that at one point, my older brother Rinji said, "They are not the orphans, we are!" But God has given her strength and grace to balance the time for us and for others.

Watching my parents interact can be very funny a times. Mummy has a different way of showing her love and affection, but Daddy is really so romantic – he's the definition of the perfect husband.

Daddy's relationship with the children that Mummy brought home is amazing. Not every African man will accept a bunch of kids into his home and love them and treat them as his own. But Daddy loves the children. There are times when I'm really tempted to tell the children to go back where they came from because they really do stress my mum. But, looking at where the children have come from and what they have gone through, I just shut up.

The Lord has been faithful. I love my family so much and I continue to pray that God will use my whole family to further his work.

Gloria on Caring for Orphans

What makes orphans into orphans is the fact that they have lost their parents. These children will not recover from their loss unless you give them what they have lost: parents. Parenting is crucial for orphans. And good parenting is about far more than giving children things or a fancy house to live in. So this is how I go about parenting the children we have adopted, many of whom come from terrible situations. Some of them have been physically and sexually abused by their loved ones and those who were supposed to take care of them. They have stolen and been stolen from. They have lied and been lied to. What Ben and I strive to do is let them see that parents are good to have. Their birth parents may not be around, but God has brought other parents into their lives to give them what they are missing. We show them what it means to be a

Christian and to be a responsible person in society today. We teach them about the joy of giving, of touching other people's lives.

We have prayers between six and seven in the morning before they go to school. I teach them that yes, Jesus rescued them from the terrible life they had before they came to live with us. But we are not supposed to live for ourselves. We are to help other people. When Jesus tells us to take his hand, he is also telling us to follow his example and live like he did.

Ben and I try very hard to apply the Bible to our daily lives and to the children's lives. We tell them that if somebody tells lies and then sits down and reads the Bible and says he or she has prayed, that person is a liar and can't be trusted. God requires us to read and obey his Word.

Sometimes when we go into local communities to distribute clothes and food, we take some of the children with us so that they can see how fortunate they are. We tell them, "You have seen for yourself how these people use the things that you have sewn and given to them. You will be blessed for doing this, because the Bible says 'it is more blessed to give than to receive' (Acts 20:35). We cannot just sit here and be receiving and receiving, because there is no joy in that."

Some of the children really struggle with these ideas, but slowly and surely, God is giving us the victory.

People think running an orphanage is just about having money and staff. But I think that even if you only have two children, it is better to invest in them by giving them love and attention than it is to have an orphanage with hundreds of kids with paid but frustrated staff and endless appeals for money.

Something else bothers me about orphanages. I have asked this question of many people, but no one seems to have an answer. Why is it that I have never seen a child from an orphanage joyfully go on to university? Perhaps they do in other countries, but in Nigeria, orphans are limited to blue-collar work. Why is that? Is there a law in Nigeria that says that a child from an orphanage cannot go to a proper school or university, but must work in tailoring or welding or jobs like that?

I have been criticized for having such high hopes for my children. But I don't care. I know where these children have come from, and I know where God can take them. They are not donkeys. They can and will learn.

So, how does Ben fit into all this?

Well, it is true to say that there is no way I could have done all these things without him. He knows the way the Spirit moves me, especially in the area of compassion for children. He has said there is nothing he can do to stop me because God has surely called me to do this work. He does joke about the fact that I have ruined his retirement plans, though ...

We are not funded by any organization or government, although we have registered the ministry as Zambiri Outreach. We did this mainly for formal reasons. Registering the ministry as a charitable organization gives me the right to walk into villages, communities and other places or situations and rescue vulnerable children. The donor who had supported the old orphanage had insisted on this, and because they are a government organization, we were able to get speedy registration.

The donor organization funded us for six months for paid staff and helped us get some of the materials we needed to get the children settled in our old house in Argak Close. But after that they gave us no more money, which was fine with me. I didn't want to be beholden to any organization that was going to dictate how I would take care of my children and drown me in paperwork. You can't put a price on love, but every time I had to file paperwork with the donor for one thing or the other, a part of me literally died. Having said all that, I have bemoaned my lack of organizational skills for years. The donor's staff really helped me with that, so I can't complain.

Zambiri is currently supported by the church of God. We have received help from Christians in Australia, the UK and Ireland who have really been wonderful. Some of them are personal friends. Others are churches to whom Ben and I have preached, and they have been touched by our ministry. Ben's younger sister, Dr Caroline Berg who lives in the USA, also supports us with regular funds.

Right now, we are the official parents of about three hundred adopted children. By the time this book is published, it's fair to say that the number will have risen. I am very well known in Jos and the surrounding states for my work with children. So every day I receive calls from people about children in crisis. Sometimes the children are brought to me. I can't take them all in, but I do try and pray that I make the right decision. Times are really hard for people. There is so much poverty in the villages that some parents and guardians just want to get rid of their responsibility and offload their children on whoever will take them. That way they will have fewer mouths to feed. So I pray and ask God to guide me to take in the children who are really at risk.

About sixty or so of these three hundred children live with us while the others are at boarding school. When the boarding students come back home, it is utter chaos. In fact, it's just mad, but I love it and wouldn't have it any other way.

Ben on Orphans and Family

It's fair to say that Gloria has ruined my retirement plans. I thought we would retire and move to a two-bedroom house. I would tinker with my beloved cars and concentrate on my writing while Gloria carried on working with women and children. But with over three hundred children and rising to feed, it is fair to say that my plan won't be happening.

When Gloria broached the subject of the children moving in with us, it never once crossed my mind to say no. It was clear that God was in this – even if I had my moments of doubt. And as anyone who has ever had the courage to say to no to Gloria eventually finds out, she wears one down. Once she has set her mind on something and is convinced that the Lord has put this thing on her heart, she doesn't give up. She says that her mind is not at rest until she finds a resolution. I say she is sometimes stubborn-headed.

But for practical reasons, it made sense to bring all forty-five or so children to live with us. Those six months of managing two homes, taking care of the children and dealing with the fallout of the whole situation exerted an emotional and physical toll on Gloria. She was exhausted. The children and I did what we could to support her, but some things only a mother can do. Like bathing the fifteen-year-old boy whose HIV-positive condition developed into full-blown AIDS. Only Gloria could have bathed him in a way that would spare him humiliation and let him know that she was his mother bathing her child, not just an adult bathing a fully grown boy.

Our womb children were great, too. Gloria kept us fully updated about the goings-on in the house, and we prayed together constantly for all the children. We would also go over whenever we could to help do whatever was needed.

As far as I could see, the transition to the main house did not pose any real issues. There were teething problems, but none that couldn't be overcome.

The move to the main house – what we now call the "mission house" – was in 2008. That was the same year in which I became an archbishop. Then we had forty-five children. We have way more than that now, and the number keeps on increasing. Word travels about Gloria's ministry with children. Now we receive calls all the time from people. They say, "Mummy Bishop, there's a child in such and such a place who needs your intervention. The child is extremely vulnerable. If you don't come and get him, we don't know what will happen to him."

And Gloria goes, as is her custom. In ways that only Gloria knows how to do, she will get documentation about the child, whether from the local village chief or the child's guardian, and then get them to sign an agreement confirming the child's name, age, place of birth, and abode and stating that they are signing over the vulnerable child to her. Child trafficking is an endemic problem in Nigeria. The last thing we want is a scandal tying the bishop's wife to such a thing. It wouldn't be a good witness for the church.

We also need the documentation for our records, so that when the children are grown up and start asking questions, we can show them the documentation. Then they can decide what to do with the information listed there.

There is also another reason I require documentation. Nigeria, for all its religiousness, is a cultic society. It is not uncommon to hear stories of children being sacrificed in some traditional ritual. Many people know of Gloria's ministry with children and that we are not supported by the government nor any international organization. They don't realize that we are supported by friends and family. So when they see our mission house and all the children running around – and no visible sources of funding for the ministry – some think we are engaged in witchcraft. So we have to be very careful with our records so that we can't be accused of such things.

Gloria and I are quite critical of orphanages. We have been caring for vulnerable children for a while now, so I believe that gives us the right to talk about the social care of children in Nigeria. We have come to the conclusion that the Catholics have exceptional levels of care in their orphanages. The Catholic sisters are well trained. Sure, their orphanages might not be as slick or glitzy as others, but they love and care for their children with the kind of love that comes from a compassionate heart and a religious conviction. From what we have seen, the workers in other orphanages are not that way inclined. As far as they're concerned, they are doing a job. They don't care about the children. They feel no affinity, no affection, no nothing. They just come, feed the children and tend to their external needs. But the real heart stuff, the love ... it's not there. I don't care where these workers are from: Europe, America, wherever. They are all the same. They attend to the children's needs. They dazzle their donors with slick buildings and expensive toys for the children. But love for the children ... that is not in those orphanages. Love is what the Catholic nuns give and what children need.

Gloria has evolved a strong theological conviction that goes like this: Love, parental love, is the essential ingredient that orphans have lost. They need people who will correct them, love them and care for them. Anyone can give them food, clothes and toys. But who can give them love and care?

I have to say that Gloria is at her best when she is with these children. In the middle of one of our never-ending "crises" in Jos, when the army has imposed a curfew, I have seen Gloria take these children to hospital at 2:00 a.m. She does not fear what the army will do if she is found on the streets at that time. I join her on these excursions – what else can I do? – because Gloria won't wait until morning when the curfew is lifted. She needs to take "my child" to hospital, and she will do it now, curfew be damned. So we pack up and get ready to go to hospital.

"Gloria, let me drive," I will say.

"No, I'm doing the driving," Gloria will reply in a clipped voice.

I know my wife, and I heed the warning signs of discord when I hear them. So I just back off. Gloria will drive to the hospital, and I will hold the child or the children. Sometimes these children are HIV-positive and in the midst of some kind of medical trauma. Sometimes the trouble is something else. We have done this a hundred times – and we are still doing it.

When the children call Gloria "Mummy," I know they mean it. If you drop by our house for a visit, and you say at the gate that you have come to visit "the orphans", some of our children will take exception. They will tell you that their names are John or Sarah Kwashi, and so on.

I've tried to get Gloria to be more practical in terms of long-term planning. But my arguments do not work, for my wife is not that way inclined.

"Ben, we have a lot to be thankful, so we shouldn't complain," she will say. "If the worst happens and we can't provide for the children, we will sell the furniture and sit on the floor. What do we need chairs for anyway? Do be quiet."

And she is right. If we can't provide for the children, we will simply sell what we have.

The children have duties and responsibilities because this is how Gloria and I were raised. Each child has a tree that he or she must water, be it a mango, guava or orange tree. They also look after the cows and monkeys and feed the dogs. Children have to be taught to be responsible. Otherwise how will they learn it? Everyone reports to me, "Daddy". I am the chief justice of the "federation", and I settle the disputes between the children.

Ours is a home, a family. I think that Gloria's theology has blessed me to think this way. Through her, I have come to believe that what these children have lost is parental love. Their greatest need is not food or money, but the kind of love they can only get from parents. Personally, we don't eat breakfast in our house, and our children – the ones Gloria birthed – don't either. But we can't continue this practice with these children. They didn't have anything growing up. So we make sure they are extremely well fed with good food and snacks. We never want them to feel different from the other children "out there".

... So, yes, Gloria has ruined my retirement plans. But that's okay. It is the way the Lord would have it.

Children wait for all to be served and a prayer said before eating

16

THE CHILDREN'S STORIES

I have many stories to tell about the children.

Take the story of one of the small boys who came to us in the first group of ten. I remember taking him to the hospital and telling the nurses he must be about four years old because he was so tiny.

The nurses checked him out. "Mummy Bishop, we've had a look at his hands and veins. He's not four. He's about seven or eight."

I was shocked into silence. But then I vaguely remembered his mother bringing him to the orphanage. She had been a sex worker with truck drivers. She contracted all kinds of sicknesses: tuberculosis and all that. She didn't know she was HIV-positive. It took a while for people to realize she was pregnant. They said that the boy was born blind and covered in pus. But gradually with medication – antiretrovirals – he got better.

Then there was the boy whom I will call David. I'm not sure of his history, and getting concrete information is hard because David has problems communicating with people. Having said that, he has come a long way in the four years he has been with us.

We found David because of a telephone call, asking us to go to the market area in Langtang, about two hours away from where we live in Jos, to pick up a boy who was wandering around the market. Nobody knew where he came from or what his name was. The villagers weren't familiar with his language. All they knew was that he had been wandering in the market for about four years and that he was naked and mad.

"How do you know that he is mad?" I asked.

No answer.

"Who are his parents and relatives?"

Again, silence. Nobody knew where he was from and they knew even less about his relatives. I wasn't surprised. Things like this happen all the time. On market days, you tend to see children just roaming around.

I had seen a situation like David's before. I wish I had been wiser then, but I genuinely didn't know that I was capable of such a ministry with children. It was when we were doing mission work, many years earlier. Every time we crossed the bridge near a village, we saw a young boy sitting there by a tree or by the stream. He was always naked – and that is how we knew he was considered mad. In the villages, the so-called mad children are always naked. Someone might have given him a pair of trousers or a shirt, but over time, the clothes would develop holes and would be worn out and discarded.

If it was raining, I would see this boy naked with nothing to cover himself with. Whatever the time of the day or night, he was always at the bridge, though on market days, he would go to the market. But he always came back to the bridge. If he was sleeping and heard a car approach the bridge, he would get up and hold the bridge railings and just look at the car. If you tried to take his picture, he would just stand and look, his eyes vacant. Or he would just turn his face away.

We tried asking the villagers about him. But they said he was mad, and that was the end of it. However, their denial had an element of shame in it, because nobody wanted to be identified as having a "mad" relative. If they did, they would have to accept responsibility for caring for him. But when the boy later died in a car accident, I found out that he did have relatives after all.

I was reminded of that little boy when I came face to face with "Gombe" as David was known in that market. Before, I wasn't wise enough to help. But now I knew I could.

When I arrived at the village, I went to David. He was sitting under a tree. I kind of waved to him and started asking the villagers questions.

"Who is he?" I asked.

"We don't know," they replied.

"Where is he from?"

"We don't know. He just appeared overnight."

"He has been like this for four years, and nobody has done anything to help him?!"

Shrug.

I was told that even if they brought food to him, sometimes he wouldn't eat it. He would stand up and just start wandering round the market. I was also told that he didn't beg. He would simply eat the leftovers that some of the market women would package up for him.

I don't believe a child can be mad. I asked the villagers if I could approach him.

"He doesn't trust us," they said. "But he may talk to you."

I got close and talked with David. He wouldn't talk, so I tried other things.

"What is your name?" I asked.

He looked at me, and then in another direction as if he was angry. But I knew that he wouldn't throw stones or harm me. So we talked a little bit – as best we could anyway – and I managed to convince David to come with me. I asked the village chief to sign him over to me, so that if we were stopped at one of Nigeria's notorious police checkpoints and they suspected us of child trafficking, I could produce the required documentation.

At the time of writing, this boy has been with us for about four years. He still has difficulty communicating, but he has come a long way. We gave him a name (here we will call him David). He is very dutiful. If you give David a task to do, like tending the plants or cleaning a room, he will do it well – so well that he will overprune the plants or bleach the room so much that it becomes uninhabitable. But ask David to count or recite the alphabet, and he will have difficulty doing either.

He has been, I admit, a huge challenge. But God has given us something to even out the challenge. When David does something that defies human understanding and you ask him why he did it, he will look at you as if you are the insane one. In those situations, remaining frustrated is very hard, and you have to laugh at yourself for forgetting that this child genuinely cannot see where he has gone wrong, and at the situation, because it's so ridiculous.

I can also tell you the story of two sisters. Let's call them Beth and Mary. Their parents died when Beth was four years old, and Mary just 18 months old. They had relatives, but nobody wanted to take responsibility for them because everyone in the village was very poor. However, an old woman took the girls in and did what she could. But it wasn't long before she took ill and died, leaving Beth and Mary on their own. Beth wanted to go to school, but she had to stay at home to look after her younger sister. The girls survived by chopping firewood and selling it to the person in the village who brewed beer. Though the girls had almost nothing, they were able to feed themselves.

By the time I heard about them, they had been living alone for more than five years. Beth was fifteen by this time. I worried about predators among the village men. How had the girls been coping? It seemed that the villagers had been keeping an eye on the girls from a distance, so they were reasonably protected, which I was really happy about.

"You really don't have any relatives to take care of you?" I asked the girls. They told me they had a grandmother in the next village. I went to see the grandmother and understood why she couldn't help: she was old and feeble.

We invited the girls to come to our home, but Beth shook her head. She insisted I take only her thirteen-year-old sister, Mary. Beth said a young boy had expressed an interest in her. She was crying as she spoke to me.

"Take my sister! Take her to school!" Beth cried. "There is no hope for me, but she has a chance. Take her! Send her to school!"

Beth got married. Three years later, I took Mary back to see her. We were approaching the village on the bus when Mary saw her sister. Beth had aged a lifetime. She was carrying a tray of basil and corn and was on her way to the village to get the corn ground so that she could sell it at the market. Mary recognized her sister and shouted, "My sister!" Then she started crying. And those were no ordinary tears.

There's also the story of another girl whom we will call Ruth (not her real name). Her mother used to sell cooked food in the market before she died. When her mother passed away, Ruth took over her mother's business. This meant that she had to buy meat from the local butcher. What she did not know was that the butcher had AIDS and had been told that he would be cured if he slept with a virgin.

Ruth was thirteen years old.

The butcher raped her.

Ruth is now sixteen years old and has been with us for a few years. She is HIV-positive and has a wonderful, gentle spirit.

The stories could go on and on. Once, when I went to my father's funeral in Numan, I came across a four-year-old who had left her eighteen-month-old sister under a tree and gone to look for something to eat. Their parents had died from AIDS, and the children had been left to fend for themselves.

I didn't have to think about what I would do. I went straight to the village head and asked if I could take the children back to Jos. Because the children had no parents, he was their legal guardian. Of course, I made sure I got all the necessary documentation.

When we read stories like these, it is easy to judge the villagers harshly. But we need to remember that poverty and hunger are very real in their lives. Many cannot afford to take in an extra mouth to feed. I am aware of this and try to balance that knowledge with educating parents and guardians about not abdicating responsibility for their children by offloading them to me, because they think it's the easy way out.

Nendelmwa's graduation from St John's College, Jos

And then ...

There's a school about twenty minutes from where we live. The principal is a devoted Christian and a real blessing from the Lord. Whenever new children join the family, I take them to the school and she enrols them. She knows that Ben and I will pay the school fees when we can afford it.

One day, I popped into the school to see the principal. As I pulled up outside the school, I saw a nice-looking young lady – very well-dressed – in a beautiful car, speaking to the principal. When the principal saw me arriving, she came over to me. I said, "Mama (that's what I call her), please finish your conversation with that lady."

"No, don't worry about it. What brings you here, again? Let me guess, you have more children for me! Don't you get tired of doing this?"

We both laughed. It was our private joke. My reply was the same as always.

"Mama, I don't know why I can't stop. But you know what I'm like: when I see someone in need, I can't stop myself! I always think that all I can do is try and help. Even if it doesn't work out, at least I know I tried."

And that's true. My brother has always said that children are like seed in your hand that you go and plant. You don't know which of those seeds will germinate, but it's up to us to do what we can for all of them. It is God who changes lives, and he can do a lot with our little.

We talked for a while about two teenagers, aged about 14 or 16, who had just come to live with us and couldn't read at all. She agreed to place them in Form One, the first year of secondary school. Then we started talking about the progress of my other children.

Suddenly, the young lady called out to the principal: "Mama, I would like to tell you something about this woman," she said, nodding in my direction.

I smiled, because I didn't want her to know that I didn't know what she was talking about.

"I'm sorry, have we met?" I asked her.

The young lady shook her head. "Mama Bishop, you've forgotten who I am. I know you have. Remember, I lived with you in Zaria."

And then I remembered.

"Mama Bishop, when you pulled up in your car, I was so happy, because, I thought, *My Mama has come!* That's why I didn't say anything when the principal went to talk to you. And when you didn't say anything to me, I thought, *My Mama doesn't remember me.*"

And then, she went on to remind me of the things she had learnt from me.

"Mama always said that no matter how hopeless a child's situation is, if you put that child in school and introduce Jesus Christ to that child, between Christ and education, the child's situation will be improved. Mama Bishop, you will be glad to know that I am now married to a pastor and we've just been transferred to Jos. I was telling myself off for leaving it so long before coming to see you. And here you are."

I had goosebumps. I didn't know what to say, so I just stood there.

"So," I managed to splutter out, "You like school now?"

"Mama Bishop, you'll be happy to know that I have put more than ten children though school."

"Glory be to God!" I said.

We started reminiscing about the past. Back in the 1980s, when we were posted to Zaria, I was outside my home looking after my pigs when I saw this beautiful young girl hanging around.

"What are you doing here? Aren't you're meant to be in school?" I asked her.

I've always been nosy.

She acted like she hadn't heard me.

"You're coming with me to my house," I commanded.

We went inside and I started talking to her.

"Look at you. Your parents work so hard, and here you are, living with a man and not going to school..."

I kept on talking to her like that. After some time, she screamed, but I carried on talking. Because in African culture, people scream for all kinds of reasons and, as far as I was concerned, she was screaming because she didn't want to hear what I was saying and wanted to distract me.

Later she told me that she thought I knew her life story because some of the things I said were spot on. I hadn't known that her father was an old man, who worked as a security guard. I was talking to her from experience. Many young girls take up with older men to survive, unbeknown to their parents. Sometimes, the parents do know about it, but choose to turn a blind eye because of their dire economic situation.

She kept on screaming and I kept on talking over her screams.

"I know you're screaming because you don't want to hear anymore. But I have to tell you: this life will not help you. It will only end in tears."

And still, she kept on crying.

To cut a long story short, we ended up fostering her. She started living with us, and eventually went back to school. It was the practical thing to do, because the last thing we wanted was for her to end up in exactly the same situation as before. Ben and I had the means to help, and so we did.

There are many stories like hers.

There was another girl, Marta, whom I picked up from a building site in Jos. She recently graduated from the University of Jos and is now married to a man with a PhD.

Marta is from the Delta region in the east of Nigeria. She came from a very humble background. There were about seven children living in the same room as their parents, so their living conditions weren't the best. Marta learnt how to sew and got hold of an old sewing machine. Her parents decided that she would earn more money with her sewing if she moved to Jos, so they basically sent her packing.

I'd started a girls' fellowship at the cathedral, which she started coming to. I noticed that, at the end of the fellowship, she would wander round like someone who didn't want anyone to know where she was going after the fellowship, and then disappear the minute she thought no one was watching her. She couldn't have been more than 16 or 17 when this happened, although it's hard to say as proof of age can be difficult to get hold of in Nigeria.

God has given me a strong instinct for spotting people in need. Sometimes it's the way they sit or look. Other times, they act overly religious, or they try very hard not to draw attention to themselves. These are warning signs of people in need, and I've been trained to look out for them. So one day, at the end of the fellowship, as people hung around to catch up with friends or to speak with me, I caught her eye. She moved away quickly. Then she waited until one of the other girls caught my attention, and quickly walked out of the cathedral. I ended my conversation with the other girl and hurried out of the cathedral and into my car. It wasn't long before I spotted her walking down the street. She knew I was following her, because she tried to turn onto a narrow footpath where a car couldn't possibly go.

I called out to her.

"Come back here."

She came.

"Where are you going?"

"I am going home," she said.

"Well, get in the car, then, and I'll take you."

She got in the car and started giving me directions.

"This way."

I would turn in the direction she told me to go.

"No, it's that way."

I would turn in that direction too.

And then, we would find ourselves in a narrow road.

"Well, a car can't go through here. Isn't there another way?" I would ask.

"Maybe, but this is the way I usually walk."

And then, I would reverse and try to find a usable road for cars. At one point, I was close to saying "Look, a car can't get in that narrow street. How about I drop you here, instead?" But I resisted, because I knew that was the reaction she was hoping for, which made me all the more determined to pursue the mystery of where she lived.

I parked the car and we started walking. Eventually, she said: "That's the house."

It was an abandoned building site that squatters had occupied. They had put cardboard to cover the holes where the windows would eventually go.

Marta didn't have a room in the uncompleted building, but she had found a space under the stairs, relatively protected from the rain. She had her little sewing machine and a kind of cotton mat that she was sleeping on. She had her food supply in there as well. You could barely stretch both your arms in that space.

I stood, shocked.

"How do you sleep?"

She demonstrated by curling up on the mat.

"Where are your parents?"

"They are 'back home' in the village."

"How did you get here?"

"My father asked around for money, gave me travel money, and sent me to Jos to sew and earn money."

"How did you discover this building? Did you know anyone...?"

My questions were endless. She said she was living somewhere else and God had "saved" her and she had started coming to church. Her story was disjointed. Or perhaps, I was the one having difficulty processing the fact that such a young girl was living on her own on a building site and had been coming to the cathedral, and no one knew how dire her situation was.

I left her for the night. But I asked her to come to the church the next day, figuring that if she didn't turn up, it was because she also worked as a prostitute and wasn't willing to give up that source of income. If that was the case, I had to think of how to help her from afar. In my years in ministry, although, I've learnt not to be surprised by what I see, I'm continually surprised.

The next day she came to the cathedral.

I'd already told Ben about her. The long and short of it was that she lived with us for about a year before going to live with our dear friend, Elizabeth, who is now with the Lord. After about two years, she found a nice young man and they got married in our house. Even though Ben and I were like her parents – we supplied everything for the wedding, and joyfully so – we insisted on meeting her real parents when she was getting married.

So, six years after she left home, Marta got married in our home. Ben and I finally got to meet her parents and, perhaps for the first time, I understood the depth of the poverty she came from, and the desperation of her father who had sent her away to another city, hundreds of kilometres away, to go and earn a living, in the hope she would have a better life.

When we first met her, she said that she had finished secondary school, but to be honest, I don't think she even went to school. With the kind of poverty in her background, I suspect she had only completed primary school, and had then been pulled out to learn sewing that would bring in money.

Today, she is a graduate. Her husband has a PhD and they have three children. She's very happy, and regardless of what anyone – or nature – might say, as far as she is concerned, Ben and I are her biological parents.

17

GOD, OUR PROVIDER

When the Bible talks about how God can make a little go a long way, I can testify that what it says is true. People genuinely don't believe that we receive no outside funding but are wholly supported by wonderful Christian friends and family.

People quite often come by and drop off clothes and toys for the children. The Mothers' Union has also been a huge help to the ministry. We document every donation and write all our supporters thank-you notes.

A prayer group helps with food for the children. One of the women in that group sold her house and gave us a share of the sale.

One day, another woman from the prayer group came to see me. I had just finished cooking and was dishing out the food for the children. She started crying.

"I am not strong enough to come and help you cook in those huge pots," she said. "But every market day, I can help by bringing some food items, vegetables, potatoes and that kind of stuff."

Her offer was such a relief – a huge burden off our shoulders.

The principal of one of the Christian schools in our area has also been very generous. Sometimes he will buy food and tell us to please keep his donation to ourselves because he doesn't want attention. But I can't do that. People have been so good and so kind to us, how can we not publicly acknowledge them?

We have also received the faithful giving of the church. Whenever Ben travels and shares the testimony about the children, people respond. A young boy once sent us £1! Each and every one of these precious people deserves to be honoured, because they really have helped us.

As for schooling the children, well, I homeschool the younger ones until they are about eleven. But I know that these children also need to go to school with other children, so that when people ask them where they went to school, they won't feel embarrassed. In Nigeria, homeschooling is viewed as inferior and only for poor children. My "womb children" did not mind being homeschooled because they understood it wasn't inferior and was a commitment I had made. I also taught my children at home because I wanted to introduce them to Jesus Christ myself.

When we travelled, my womb children would say, "I am going to school at home. My mother is my teacher." Their voices were filled with pride. However, my new children are coming from backgrounds that tend to give them an inferiority complex. So when they reach the age of eleven or twelve, we send them to secondary school with the other children in the community. Some of the schools are boarding schools (we have strong relationships with some schools in Jos and they take in our children – we pay what we can in fees) and some are local, secondary schools.

Ben and I have also built a number of community schools. Anytime we receive a huge gift from friends of the ministry, we put the money towards building a school.

Finding the land is relatively easy. I go on my walking expeditions, and if I see a piece of suitable land, I approach the local elders and start bargaining.

I tell them, "I want to build a school here for this community. So, how can we work together? If you reduce the cost of this land for us, in return you will receive a good education for the children in this community."

This is how Ben and I have managed to build about sixteen community schools. Most are in Jos. Some are outside Jos, in places whose names I can't even remember!

God has also blessed us with a great business. I had prayed to God for a wafer-making machine so that I could supply communion wafers to the churches, and also use the proceeds to help the widows in the church. I didn't know it would become a big money-making venture! I just thought it would be useful to the church. Well, I was blessed with a wafer machine, and now the business supplies three big denominations in Jos. Profits from the sales of the wafers help both widows and orphans.

I have also taught the older children how to use the machine so they make the wafers when they come home for holidays, so it's a bit like their holiday job.

When the older children finish secondary school, some of them go on to further studies, while others find jobs and move out of the mission house. But I keep in touch with all of them. When they come by and visit, it's such a joy because they can see for themselves how far God has brought them.

Zambiri School: Children at lunch in the Feeding Centre

HANNATU'S EPILOGUE

When people ask me, "What does it feel like to be a bishop's daughter?" I really don't know because I have always seen my parents as pastors, and ministering is what they love to do.

I'm back in Nigeria now. In the hospital where I work, once people find out I'm Bishop Kwashi's daughter, they treat me with respect. They don't just say, "Oh, this is the bishop's daughter." They tell me how good my parents are or how much they admire them. They tell me the things I know and see about my parents.

I think my parents are a beautiful couple. I don't know how to explain it, but I know I am privileged and blessed to have parents like them. I keep praying to God, I want my children and, if possible, my children's children to see my parents. I don't want my children to just hear my parents' story. I want them to see and experience it for themselves.

My parents are a beautiful couple. I thank God for their lives every day.

GLORIA'S EPILOGUE

When I think of the circumstances of my birth, life in my village of Numan, and the three months I spent in hospital as a twenty-one-year-old girl tending my cancer-ridden mother, I am so thankful to God for doing far above anything I could ever ask or even think of receiving from him.

I didn't think I would get married because I didn't believe that such a joyous, good thing could happen to a dark-skinned, ugly girl like me. But God gave me Ben, a man with a heart that burns with passion for God and people – and the ability to make me laugh! We have been married for over thirty years, and I still maintain that no one can make me laugh like he can. But even he will admit that he wasn't expecting to be the father of over 300 children when he proposed to me in seminary all those years ago.

In all, I wouldn't trade my life for anything. My name is Gloria. God's daughter. Mother. Archbishop's wife.

Rescued orphans brought home to Argak Close

Playground at Gidan Kauna, the official home of the Bishop of Jos

NIGERIA

African countries are by their nature rather complex. But Nigeria, with more than 250 ethnic groups, each with its own language, customs and political complexity, must be an anthropologist's and sociologist's dream – or nightmare, depending on the way you look at it. (Even the exact number of ethnic groups is hotly debated – estimates vary from 250 to 370 to 500!)

Nigeria borders on Benin, Niger, Chad and Cameroon. With a population of 170 million and rising, it is the most populous country in Africa. UNICEF says that one in every five Africans is Nigerian.

The eastern and southern parts of Nigeria, including Lagos, the commercial capital, have often been classified as Christian and the north as Muslim – but this represents a gross over-simplification. There has long been an active Christian community in the north of Nigeria. However, the constant portrayal of that region as Muslim, played out against a background of competing political, financial and ethnic interests, has contributed to the rise of a new breed of Nigerians. They profess an Islamic faith and use terrorism to threaten the Christian minority in the north and to hold the whole country to ransom. Meanwhile the region suffers from high illiteracy, high infant mortality, and many other problems.

This is the context in which Ben and Gloria Kwashi carry out their ministry in Jos.

Although this book focuses on Gloria, Ben Kwashi has also had a remarkable career. He has played an active role in the affairs of the Anglican Communion in Nigeria and internationally, particularly through EFAC, the Evangelical Fellowship of Anglican Communion, an organization started by John Stott.

Lightning Source UK Ltd.
Milton Keynes UK
UKHW020507020621
384753UK00006B/196